HILTON HEAD ISLAND

# Sea Change

# HILTON HEAD ISLAND
# Sea Change

*Edited by:*

James A. Mallory
Susan Riley
Hiyaguha Cohen
Denise Spencer
LA Winkle
Sharron Sypult
Gloria Krolak
Eric Johnson

Cover Photo by: Rick VanDette, used by permission.
Layout & Design: Iconix Digital Arts

An Island Writers Network Anthology
Hilton Head Island, SC

A project of
The Island Writers Network
Hilton Head Island, SC
www.islandwritersnetworkhhi.org

ISBN: 979 83 4353 102 2

Printed in the United States of America
First Printing

# Dedicated to:

Bill Newby
IWN Moderator (2017-2019)

His leadership, coaching, and writing have inspired many.

# Acknowledgments

Island Writers Networks' anthologies are always a mixture of thoughts, moods, and memories. We chose the title *Sea Change* because, in our poems and stories, we often tell of "profound or notable transformation" or write about changes in our lives or our characters' lives. Life is about seeing and experiencing change. As one editorial board member said, the title "evokes the island spirit, reflects societal shifts, and demonstrates growth as writers." Shakespeare used the words *Sea Change* in *The Tempest* to illustrate literal transformation by the sea ... "But doth suffer a sea change into something rich and strange." The Lowcountry attracted a lot of us because we wanted a change in our lives. Finally, the name commemorates our twenty-five-year history and the changes our organization has experienced.

*Sea Change* features prose and poetry by 29 writers and photos from 10 photographers. In our 8th anthology, writers share memories of childhood, family, and friends. They tell stories that challenge the imagination. Sea change was not given as a prompt, but many of our writers wrote about transformation. The photography captures scenic images of the Lowcountry and the creatures that live in the trees, marshes, and waterways.

We gratefully acknowledge the creativity and dedication of our members who submitted their works to us and the editorial board members who gave up weeks of their summer to edit and mentor our contributors. Sadly, this is the first of our eight anthologies to not have the editing talent and insight of Sansing McPherson, who passed in 2023. She was, and continues to be, missed.

We nod thanks to members of the Photography Club of Sun City Hilton Head and Hilton Head photographer Lindsay Pettinicchi. Their visual artistry once again enhances our anthology.

~*Eric Johnson, IWN Moderator*
~*James A. Mallory, Chair of the Editorial Board*

# Contents

## Rebuilding

## Evolution

# Variations

# Renewal

# SHIFTS

*Mag'nole* | Julie Kimmel

# Rainshine

Barry Dickson

This was at least the tenth time I noticed the remarkable phenomenon. It was raining behind my house, but not in front. Each time this happened, I was sitting in my office looking out the back window: pouring. Front window: sunshine.

I told myself it must be the way Hilton Head Island is situated. It's a barrier island separated from the mainland by about a mile, and that mile must affect the way air currents and storm fronts travel the length of the island's sneaker shape. That Hilton Head is almost perfectly dissected by Broad Creek might help explain. Or maybe the way Calibogue Sound and Port Royal Sound converge.

I researched as much as I could. I even wrote to the National Weather Service. They gave no insight specific to Hilton Head but did offer several explanations of rain in one spot but not the other. They even sent videos.

In any case, I considered myself lucky that my house, on the ninth hole of Dolphin Head Golf Course, happened to be in a place where it rains outside one window but not the other.

One day, while I was working on a poem at my desk, it happened again. Same phenomenon!

I called out to my girlfriend, Kathy, who was reading in the sunroom.

"Look!" I said, pointing outside. "It's raining on one side of the house and not the other!"

She looked toward the back and then leaned forward to get a good look through a front window.

I went on. "This happens all the time!"

"Uh, Barry ..." she said.

"It's like about the fifteenth time I've seen ..."

"Barry ..." she interrupted.

"What?" I said, a bit annoyed she wasn't sharing my enthusiasm.

"... that's not rain. That's the sprinkler system on the golf course. I see it here a lot. Usually this time of day."

I looked out the back window and then the front.

"Hmph," I said. "Darn National Weather Service didn't mention that one."

*Rain* | Rick VanDette

# Ridge Road

Susan W. Harris

I sat on our couch after dinner reading the latest bestseller by Morris West, The Shoes of the Fisherman. Jerry and I were enjoying the surrounding solitude of our comfortable cottage. I watched my husband of a year sitting across from me as he opened his briefcase to read hospital reports. Then he raised his head as if he heard something.

Suddenly, we heard a woman yelling, "Help. Help me please. Help!" as she banged on the front porch door. Jerry rushed to the front door and turned on the porch light. The light revealed a hysterical woman with her hands bound in front of her.

"He's out there. He has a knife!" she screamed.

We looked at each other, confused. Our instinct was to help, but our wariness of danger made us pause. In seconds, we nodded to each other, and he went out to the porch and opened the door.

She was wide-eyed.

We hurried her inside, steering her to the couch. She peeked out our large bow window and whispered, "He's out there."

I yanked the café curtains closed but realized they only covered the bottom four feet. I bent over so my head wouldn't show from the outside and crept around the room.

Jerry called the police and got heavy scissors to cut the cords that bound her wrists. I brought her a glass of water. She trembled as she drank.

She told us her name was Marie Caruso.

Of medium height and build, she appeared to be in her mid-twenties. Her hair was black. She had brown eyes and olive skin. Thankfully, the police arrived in ten minutes. Jerry explained the situation to them, and Sgt. Mallory and Detective Clark immediately searched the area around our house, but found no one. They took her personal information and learned that she lived in Highwood, a suburb adjacent to our town, Highland Park.

"Please describe your experience," said Detective Clark.

"My girlfriend, Shirley, and I were at the Parkside bar in Highland Park and met a man, Tom, who offered to buy us a drink. Shirley decided to move on after the first one, but Tom persuaded me to stay and offered to give me a ride home."

"He had a gray 1960 Ford sedan. He started toward Highwood but then detoured and ended up on Ridge Road. I protested, but he ignored me."

"He turned into a wooded dirt drive. Smiling, he said, 'Nice and private.'"

"From underneath his seat, he pulled some cord and a knife. He bound my wrists and unzipped his pants."

"I panicked. With my knee, I pushed up the car door handle and shoved open the door with my body. I tumbled out and started to run. Seeing lights from this house at the bottom of the hill, I ran toward them."

"What did he look like?' asked the detective.

"He was short and had black hair and brown eyes."

Detective Clark said to us, "We know the Lover's Lane spot on the hill above you. We try to patrol it, but not on a regular basis."

"We will take you home, Miss," said Sgt. Mallory.

Detective Clark turned to us, "We may need to go over your property tomorrow."

"I will be here until 10:00 a.m.," said Jerry.

Distraught, we ended up talking through the night. Our idyllic world was punctured. We felt invaded. What began as a peaceful, relaxing evening ended with chaos and crime.

෫෮

We were married the year before, in 1962, and were ecstatic to rent a little cottage on a country estate close to the hospital where Jerry worked. It was located in Highland Park on Ridge Road, about thirty miles north of Chicago. Ridge Road was a lonely macadam road with dense woods on either side, and several long driveways led to secluded estates. Our rental, the gardener's cottage, was part of a fifteen-acre estate that included the main house, horse stables, a greenhouse, and tennis courts. The cottage had a tiny kitchen, two small bedrooms, a living room, and an attached, screened front porch. The living room featured a floor-to-ceiling, large bow window overlooking long-forgotten and unkempt formal gardens. It was about thirty yards across the driveway from the main house. It had sat empty for nearly a decade, but we were enraptured by it. We cleaned it up and made it ours. We never expected what might happen beyond our enchanted cottage.

We watched dawn break the next morning. Not having slept, we were drinking our umpteenth cup of coffee when Detective Clark arrived. He said, "We checked out the Parkside bar, and nobody remembered anybody fitting his or her description."

"Jerry," he said, "would you do me a favor? Put on your sneakers and come with me."

Jerry looked quizzically at me, and I hunched my shoulders in question.

The detective drove on Ridge Road toward the hill above us and turned onto the dirt lane.

I waited at the bottom of the hill and watched the detective instruct Jerry to put his hands together in the front. It looked like they were bound. The detective did the same. He said something, and they ran down the hill toward our house.

After stumbling down through the old formal gardens and

falling into potholes and ruts, they made it.

"Now look at your shoes," the detective said.

Jerry's sneakers were covered in grass and dirt. His pants were dirty.

"This tells me that woman did not run down this hill. Her sneakers were white with no grass or dirt. Her jeans were clean. You and I had trouble running down the hill in the daylight. She said she ran down the hill last night. SHE NEVER DID!"

"What do you think happened?" asked Jerry.

"We think that it was a setup for an attempted robbery. But ... they got the wrong house. They mistook your house for the main house. Since the owners were away on vacation, your house had the only lights. When she got inside your house, she realized her mistake. No insult meant, ma'am."

I assured him none was taken.

"He was probably waiting for her signal but took off when he saw our police car. We will continue to question her. But with no crime committed, we can't charge her. We will also keep your house and this property under surveillance for a while, though I don't think they will try anything here again."

After the detective left, Jerry and I walked back inside. We realized our naïveté in believing our beloved cottage insulated us from the realities of life. However, looking back fifty-one years later, I cherish the year we had in our idyllic world.

# Generations of Discontent

Phil Lindsey

Peter Pan from Neverland
and I from down the street
did not grow up together
though often-times we'd meet
on the playgrounds of our childhood
in the backyards of our youth
in fields where fun and fantasy
transcended facts and truth.

Sunday teachers taught us
right and wrong were well-defined.
The *good guys* mostly wore white hats
and would not cross the line.
I suppose the games we played back then
were politically incorrect
but politics was for adults
we meant no disrespect.

One day Jackie Paper
said he didn't want to play.
Peter Pan got angry
took the ball and ran away.
Carrie Anne was playing
a new and different game.
Dylan told us times were changing
soon nothing was the same.

At Woodstock, Country Joe asked,
*What're we fightin' for?*
Our brothers, friends and classmates
were shipped out and sent to war.
We grew apart together;
wore different colored hats.
And as everyone was smiling
we disappeared like Cheshire cats.

Now, the generations after us:
Millennials, Xs, Zs
are grown and want to drive the car.
They *demand* to have the keys.
Will the roads they choose to travel
follow pre-existing routes?
Or will they trust their GPS,
and throw our old maps out?

Childhood games are packed in storage.
We go to dinner, watch TV.
Sometimes we reminisce a bit
about how things used to be.
We wonder what has happened
since the Boomers lost control;
We see discontent and anger,
increasing vitriol.

Somewhere, Peter Pan is laughing,
and continues playing games.
The more that things are different,
the more they stay the same.

# Varady's Grove

Gloria Krolak

Before the chainsaws cut down the trees, before the bulldozers tore into my friends' sturdy stone home, Varady's Grove was a sanctuary to the neighborhood children. By neighborhood I mean the first tract of many that signaled the change from a farming community to the crowded suburb of Fords, New Jersey.

Directly out of Newark, our new house sat across the street from Varady's Grove, a twenty-or-so-acre plot owned by an old Hungarian man we knew only as Varady. It was summertime, and it wasn't long before my brother Kenneth made friends with Varady's grandson John, another 10-year-old. Once our mother discovered John had a sister, he was made to bring me along. Janet was six to my eight, but we could pass for agemates. She became my best friend, although I never went inside her house or she in mine. Their parents, also part of the Varady household, had little contact with anyone outside the grove, as we would learn.

The grove became playground to about a dozen other children whose names are mostly lost to memory. At the southern end of the property were the woods, a respite of shade and dappled sun and a tranquility new to city dwellers. In contrast, secret hiding places encouraged the boys in their perennial fighting games. Someone had roped an old tire to one of the trees fording a shallow creek. The boys were improving their "survival skills" for some future battle. Girls forged hiking trails, ran through tunnels of thickets, each clearing becoming a room in our grand house. The cache of amber depression-era glass we found was tinged with real gold, or so we thought. For us, it was a eureka moment, not someone's spring cleaning.

One day, though, we found empty beer bottles along a path, a discovery we knew would have confirmed our parents' fears—had we told them—that vagrants and troublemakers who might harm us were in the woods. But we could not equate bad people harming us simply because they drank beer since our own fathers did too. Plus, the consequence of being forbidden to play in the grove was too horrid to contemplate. So, we kept the information to ourselves.

Beyond the woods to the north was the broad field where ballgames of all kinds and new kinds were played. Sometimes the grasses in the field grew long enough to flop into. Other times, they were roughly trimmed and sweet smelling. Rules were made, broken, and remade. Conflicts were often solved with the ball's owner going home, only to return the next day as if there had been no disagreement. John's dad built him a go-kart and let Kenneth drive it, a highlight of his boyhood. Varady's Grove was not Utopia. With the exceptions of street games like tag and dodgeball, boys and girls rarely played together. There were squabbles—fights over the tire swing and enough "I-was-here-firsts" on any ordinary day. But no one got seriously hurt or called in parental reinforcements.

While the boys played raucously in the field, we girls were often climbing on one of the ten or so apple trees that lined the east side of the field. We sat in the trees—one had a horizontal branch like a bench that was strong enough to hold three skinny kids—eating apples by the armfuls, despite having been warned not to. They would cause upset stomachs, our mothers warned. I never claimed an apple-induced bellyache despite eating four or five at a time. We ate them green because the intoxicating fragrance enticed us to eat them before they ripened. Another secret well-kept.

Further north were the man-made structures like the barn small enough for us to climb its roof for a bird's eye view. First one up was the Ruler of the Realm. Picnic tables were spread under the shade trees, sometimes used as obstacle courses for jumping on or over and climbing under, spiderwebs notwithstanding. Rail fencing around the barn became our horses traveling across the western U.S. or camels in the driest deserts.

Then there was the covered band pavilion. Across the top of the stage, the lyrics of a once-popular song were written in flowery cursive: "Enjoy Yourself. It's Later Than You Think." When Janet's mother called for John and her to come inside for supper, we knew it was later than we thought. Once in the rectangular pavilion, we danced and ran in circles on the wooden floorboards until we were breathless. Some roller-skated, wearing the kind attached to shoes and tightened with a key. We pretended we were performers on the stage, as loud as we wanted, as there was no one living close enough to complain. Not far away was a toolshed, long and low like a chicken coop—windows so dusty you could barely see inside. No matter. We knew the shed was off-limits.

Our friends' old house was in the center of the grounds on a crest that today supports four homes back-to-back. The front door led into a bar that I imagined had been the living room. I saw the interior only once during a picnic when the heavy door opened, and I could peek inside. It was dimly lit with men inside smoking, talking, and drinking from liquor bottles along a wall.

The best times were the Sunday Hungarian picnics, as they were advertised. The band of children who regularly played in the grove was neither welcomed nor discouraged from enjoying the music, local fresh corn, and paprika-spiced chicken. We seemed invisible to the adults. The band shell then came alive with a real band, including a tuba. Women in colorfully embroidered and polka-dotted dresses with swirling skirts danced in ways we would later try to imitate. The men wore dress pants held up by suspenders. We knew the music originated from far away, that it was special to the dancers, that it could cause tears of homesickness.

One warm September afternoon, we came home from school and ran into our rooms to shed school uniforms for playclothes, as was our habit. I waved to my grandmother as I ran past her. She had come to live with us and claimed her favorite spot by the picture window in the living room. She had been watching the industrious old man chopping trees for most of the day. "It's too much," she said, "too much for an old man like him." Before the sun began to fall, he had collapsed to the leafy ground. Kenneth discovered his body.

The drama unfolded before my family like a feature movie. Police directing cars, ambulance lights pulsing, people running from, to, and in all directions seeking and offering help. I was saddened for my friends and thought it somehow unjust that we knew of John and Janet's grandpa's death before they did. Worst of all, we were never to see our friends again. Their family moved away without a goodbye. The grove had been sold for yet another tract of houses.

Saws cried against chestnut and elm branches. Walnut and oak trunks thudded heavily to the ground. These became familiar but not welcome sounds. Beeches and birches, once gracious landlords, were forced to evict birds and squirrels. The promise of long-lived hickories would not be fulfilled. Gone was the view from my bedroom window of cypress and black ash in their spring baby greens, dusty summer attire, and fall spectacle of true living colors. Skinny aspen that once waved their greenery at me in the breeze—all gone.

Instead, there was a deep scar I could see, feel, and smell. I could hear the emptiness by the sound of cars going by at night. Barrenness and open sky had replaced a nearly adult-free playground where imaginations were unconstrained. Where we reveled in the use of our bodies for climbing, running, and jumping. Where there were joy, laughter, and intention. After the destruction and removal of all but the dirt, earth-moving equipment bullied the clay-tinged soil to the new owner's orders. The U-shaped driveway was to be named Varady Drive, a choice from which we would derive no comfort.

Change was coming to Fords. Varady and his family were the first to feel it. They'd lost their private retreat to the suburbs knocking on their door. John disdained Lafayette Estates as "cheese boxes on a raft," a phrase he likely heard from his adults. We were the interlopers, and there were many more to come. Even ponds on which we had all skated would be erased with dirt dug for new basements.

Years later, in middle school, I visited a classmate who lived in a house where Varady's apple trees once stood. As I looked out her bedroom window and saw the barren backyard, I could feel my mother's cautions about apples causing bellyaches coming true.

*Unsplash* | Alexandra Cozmei

# The Woman in Pearls

James A. Mallory

*In observance of the 20th Anniversary*
*of September 11, 2001*

A clear blue sky frames
a banking plane's silhouette.
Not a small one.
Pilot off track?
No.
A jetliner.
A new weapon
of mass destruction.
A first image
of September 11, 2001.

Smoke, flames, and death.
Heroes rush into eternity.
Masses fleeing America's iconic city,
as if a B-movie horror
was right on their heels.
A symbol of might and wealth imploded.
But this was not cinema.
It foretold a changing world.

Of all the images
from that *New Day of Infamy*
one resonates.
Twenty years later.

The young black woman in pearls,
her shocked look, gray soot from head to toe.
She was sharp when she arrived at work,
just minutes before her life changed.
As did ours.

Neither the photographer nor she could know
that image would forever
immortalize an attack
that killed more than 3,000.

She survived that day.
But not in spirit.
They say she never
overcame the horror.

Drugs and alcohol
dulled her pain.

A dozen or so years later, at 42,
stomach cancer did
what the terrorists didn't
the day they made her,
one of many images
we remember from
September 11, 2001.

# Beginnings

Sharron Sypult

Every great love story begins with a beginning. As Jim told it, he fell in love the first time he laid eyes on me—barefoot and chewing tobacco in the hills of West Virginia.

There's no telling what Jim added over the years in retelling this story. He had a way of embellishing on the spot. He probably said I had pigtails and wore bib overalls. He probably said I was sitting in the middle of a winding dirt road down some hollow with a hound dog named Buster or Bark Twain, fixin' to go fishin'. There is a smidgen of truth in there.

As a child, I did fish with Markie Freeland in a fishing hole at the end of a pasture of cow patties as thick as pancake batter. One afternoon, a *bull* with no horns chased us up a tree and refused to leave. We whooped and hollered, but that cow remained steadfast. I yelled, "Shoo, Bessie! Shoo!" (I had to name her something.) We hurled branches at Bessie, peanut butter sandwiches, and every single thing in the bag slung on my back, but the beast was committed. She swatted flies with her tail and looked at us with demented cow eyes trying to figure us out. I don't know how long we were treed, but it got dusky and then nearly dark before Markie's older brother was sent to fetch us. We were grateful for the fetching. I didn't fish much after that and never caught much anyway. My fish story turned into a cow story, and I learned to expect the unexpected in storytelling.

I did wear pigtails and some borrowed cut-off shorts to a Sadie Hawkins Day dance. I went barefoot because of the school rule: "Don't ever wear shoes in the gymnasium because they will scratch the floor." No one dared question the rule or learn the punishment, a detail I considered important. One thing was certain: Catching a husband was the furthest thing from my mind. I was just trying to survive in a house full of unruly, rambunctious hellions ... I mean kids.

My strikingly beautiful mother with the softest blue eyes became a widow at 34 or 35. She was born at home, and there's always been confusion as to when. Without a birth certificate, she didn't exist ... legally. After graduating from high school, she married a man in the army and thereby qualified for military benefits, but first, her father had to verify her date of birth. Here's the murky part. He either forgot when she was born or claimed she was older or younger than she was. There's no way of telling, but whatever he swore became her official age—16 or 17 or 15. Two things are certain: Never ask a woman her age ... or weight.

As I was saying, Mom had five children to feed, clothe, and control. She shared whatever she had, welcomed anyone who showed up for dinner, and laughed at Betty Boop's "boop-oop-a-doop." I learned much later that Boop, a cartoon character, is a sex symbol and slightly risqué. Her signature phrase represents virginity, and her childlike voice belies a full-on, in-your-face, unashamed sexuality. It's delightful how naive children can be.

At any rate, Mom wore red lipstick and never left the house undone. At Christmas, she knitted us sweaters, cooked enough for an army, and sang and danced like nobody's business. I can still feel the love and laughter that radiated from her soul and hear her singing, "Alice, Where Are You Going?" We answered, "Upstairs to take a bath." The song ends when Alice pulls the plug and slides down the tub hole with a "Glub. Glub. Glub." I didn't think on it much, but going down the drain gave me the heebie-jeebies.

Mom also sang "Crazy" by Patsy Cline. I wondered if my mother felt crazy for loving someone and if I could ever leave home and her behind.

I had an idyllic childhood except for the dysfunctional part. We were not the poorest of the poor, but I wore my brothers' hand-me-downs. Black galoshes were fine for the boys but not for me. Mom bought clothes at Gabs (short for Gabriels). We called it "Gab-re-ELL-ES" to give it class. She also bought slightly dented and almost out-of-date cans of food at a store in an alley full of stones and potholes difficult to navigate. None of that mattered much, but deodorant would have been a godsend for all parties concerned.

Occasionally, we bought a dozen hot dogs for a dollar at Myers Park Drug Store—with onions and meat sauce. At least, I think it was meat. Yann's, a popular hot dog spot, set in motion a family rite of passage: Adults and children alike had to swallow a blazing-hot Yann's dog without wincing or tearing or choking, no matter the age, even if the throat and lips burned for hours—which happened only always. Then Yann's shut down amid rumors they used horsemeat to make their sauce. Months later, it reopened with business as big as all get out. I still hanker for a Yann's hot dog.

Mom was a former head cheerleader, so I became a head cheerleader. "Get an education," she always said. "They can't take that away from you." What was taken from her, I could only guess. How I could afford college, I didn't know. Women in our family usually married young and aged quickly.

Be that as it may, this is a story about Jim, not Mom. It's as easy as apple pie to get sidetracked in telling the story. Contrary to Jim's account, I was not barefoot or chewing tobacco when I first laid eyes on him. Everyone was milling around outside after lunch at East Fairmont High School when I heard a deep, booming voice call "Cheri," my nickname. I spun about-face, and there he stood, six-three, athletic with broad shoulders, a disarming grin and dimple in his chin, the handsomest boy I ever saw. I was smitten. I took a deep breath and listened to my heart. I loved Jim the moment we met. I love him now and every minute in between.

"Hi," I said, which I might have pronounced with two syllables. (For the longest time, I also said "crick" instead of "creek.")

"Hi," he said. Words went out the door. We were alone in a

crowd of people with a delicious light shining through the trees. I had the presence of mind to offer Jim a bite of my candy bar. He went home that day and told his mother he met the girl he was going to marry. And that was that, a life-changing moment that happened in an eye blink.

Sometimes, someone unexpectedly shows up out of nowhere and changes the state of affairs. My life and love became one and the same. Whatever it was, it was wonderful, a powerful force, a love beyond reason. Jim was naturally funny and had a certain magic, charisma, a je ne sais quoi. His dad loved football, so Jim became a star quarterback and captain of the football team and later captain at West Virginia University. Football was his life; and cheerleading mine. It wasn't the football star who captured my heart, though; it was Jim. He loved to read and write and always kept journals. He told funny stories and sent me handwritten notes: "You are my heart," e.g., and "God smiled on me the day you came into my life." He was the editor of the school paper; I was a reporter. He was the class president; I was the freshman homecoming attendant. He was the prince; I was the princess.

Ball games, sock hops, a hayride, and first kiss later, Jim asked me to go steady, which meant we dated exclusively. He drilled a hole in a football cleat, and I proudly wore it on a chain around my neck—announcing to the world I was his girl. I felt seen and exactly where I was meant to be.

His hands engulfed mine, and I fit perfectly in the hollow of his arm. His eyes—steady, intense, seductive. I ached to be near him, with him. The mere touch of him set me afire. I gave Jim my heart and soul, and he did in-kind. At 14, I was swept away and as happy as I'd ever been. A love like ours happens but once, if at all, and usually at a young age.

Our families we couldn't sweep away. My 7-year-old brother spied on us from behind a sofa. Jim bribed him with quarters to make the little dickens go away. My middle brother sat in the living room cleaning a 12-gauge shotgun when Jim arrived for a date. *Sweet Jesus!* The football coach reminded Jim of an athletic scholarship at WVU hanging in the balance. Our parents decided we needed to date other people. We did, but an invisible force pulled us together like magnets. Without love, life is just blank pages.

Despite the roadblocks, we were as idealistic as youth allows, full of dreams and possibility and unalterable passion. As soon as Jim got his driver's license, he wanted to park—code for kiss and caress in a parked car, alone—and I was all for it. I heard about parking, but this was my first reconnaissance. Jim drove his dad's station wagon down a rural road to God knows where in the boonies. It was a light night, and stars sparkled overhead—perfect and ours for the taking. We parked and were in the moment ... necking.

Soon after, and out of nowhere, a bright light like a squad car lit up the night. We stopped dead in our tracks. We were caught red-handed and in a heap of trouble.

*Game over,* I thought. *Arrest? Jail? What will Mom say?*

I heard a hum, a rumble, a loud clickety-clack, clickety-clack, clickety-clack. Then a whistle—more like a toot—another toot, and then a long shrill blast. My heart was racing and my life changed— factors often brought on by cops.

Our car began to vibrate and subsequently shake like a son of a bitch. The steady chugging gave way to a powerful force and whooshing, whooshing, whooshing. Just as suddenly, as if a light switched off, the black dark returned. It was not our be-all and end-all, after all.

We sat motionless, blinking in the dead of night, Jim holding me close, my heart beating out of my chest. We paused in reflection. I did not hear or see the train until it was upon us. I heard Jim curse for the very first time. Until then, he never used a word that wasn't in the Bible. He took a deep breath and got out to determine how close we came to dying.

"How close?" I asked.

"Close," he said, "but no cigar." Funny never gets old.

I don't know how many inches exactly, but we had parked dangerously close to a railroad track. Our parking days came to an end before they got started. After that, I found drive-in theaters more to my liking. By the grace of God, we survived a train smushing us like marshmallows and people trying to break us up. Some magnetic force brought us together, and my destiny was linked to his forever and a day.

# Houseguests

Jeanie Silletti

exhausted by a constant bed and breakfast
alarmed by phone calls with yet more bookings
burdened by hefty Publix receipts
fearful I might run out of wine

nervous dinners may not be gourmet
concerned flights could get delayed
horrified cleaners won't appear on time
fearful I might run out of wine

bored with tours to same locations
upset by politics that accompany dinner
dismayed at forecasts of rainy days
fearful I might run out of wine

renewed by time with cherished friends
calmed by beach walks and shared moments
thankful for heartfelt notes and gifts
no longer fearful I might run out of wine

# Little Resurrections

Elizabeth Robin

A click, a pause, a sudden sharp and unexpected shock. She'd been perusing her email SENT archives in search of proof a client had signed off on her copy. Somehow, she'd landed in 2007, seen her brother's address, and automatically selected it. This retrieval of little pieces of their relationship had become a habit in the last three months. At odd moments, she'd think of a photograph from some family trip and find herself systematically pulling out and sifting through musty albums and piles of loose photographs from her old school pencil box. The ones she'd thrown in there as rejects. Too blurry. Too silly. Too many of the same pose.

Now, each one expands in meaning, its significance grown immeasurably.

As she reads the email, sobs escape. Unbidden. Uncontrollable. She's been seized by these kinds of fits often, randomly, and each time feels surprise at how fresh her sorrow feels.

The email didn't say much. Anything, really. A banal, albeit peppy exchange that seven years ago represented their communications. Weekly updates, between visits that always felt too sparsely spaced and remarkably brief. That week he'd been to a Red Sox game, looked forward to their impending visit. She'd been to see her son in Paris, regaled him with her younger daughter's softball season, her older daughter's new job. Both reflected no understanding of what they would soon lose. They wrote as if their lives would go on forever. Or at least for decades.

She thinks again of what he has already missed. The birth of his first grandchild, just two months after his death. She knows the order of these events is providential. The close of one tragic chapter, neatly and well before the opening of an exciting, fresh one. Even so, this fact stings. She finds if she thinks about it, fresh tears well up. She looks to the sky. Why she always refers upward to speak to her family she has never understood, long past the ability to believe in any afterlife, any spiritual being directing the many horrors that unfold in this world. To trust this belief would be to confirm a quixotic, sometimes malicious force. Even so, she looks up each time anyone in the family flies and asks her pilot father to watch over them. When her brother's diagnosis offered a 17 percent chance of hope, she looked up to her mother to pull him through. Each parent held a special jurisdiction. Her mother's realm for the most part was her children; she had always recognized her mother's rabid protectiveness toward them, and especially her brother. A certainty possessed her that if he had any hope, she was advocating viciously for recovery *up there.*

A bitter laugh accompanies this thought. And yet, she now consults *up there* to relate to her brother how dearly his new family member snuggles into her arms, how solid and alive she feels. How she has his cheeks, his cowlick, but his son-in-law's nose, hands, and feet. Most of all, how beautifully his daughter has assumed motherhood with a radiance and practicality that are her nature. He has been cheated of this joy, yet she understands the price he paid to remain, even as long as he did, was untenable. This man who fought so valiantly to live has earned his place *up there,* and she will not corrupt his belief in the existence of a place that enfolded him when he left her here.

Even so, this idea brings her no peace. She feels as untethered today, reading this email of a time when tragedy, for once in her life, distanced itself, as she ever has. Nothing anchors her to that past anymore, reminds her in any situation of who she should be. Now she relies on herself, her own memory, the final eyewitness to that ideal family she lost so long ago. For sixty years, he had been her sole confidante, she, his final consult, especially when parents or friends or spouses were a poor audience. Bonded by childhood romps and an early tragedy, brother and sister held a comfortable, reliable counsel. They had never held secrets from one another.

But this bond is not what she misses at this moment, looking at the terse pleasantries here. The pang of emptiness and despair stems from that normalcy, a vacuum in little happenings they'd banter about on the phone. She knows she slammed him for his Red Sox allegiance in their next conversation. Having married a Yankee fan, she peppered their rivalry with sports talk. She would have related the fabulous museum she lost herself in for a day, and he'd wonder how she could find anything that could take so long. She'd mention their little picnics of wine and cheese on the floor of her son's apartment, and he'd remain silent, a tacit disapproval. They'd always been opposites in so many ways, and yet their differences never mattered. Their moral compass remained uniform, always. Any conversation could move quickly from these differences to serious matters where the other knew exactly what to say. How he felt. What she needed.

It is hard for her to imagine at this moment how she can continue without him, yet she knows she must. This exact process runs through her head in a repeating loop each time some odd photograph, email, phone call, or memory resurrects him. She knows from experience how familiar this loop will become, a third unraveling thread from the tapestry that stitched her childhood together. She berates herself for wallowing, reminds herself how lucky her life has been. The love and certainty in each other that was her family cement her strength, her ability to survive. She lives truly happy, content in her choices, husband, and children because of that foundation. Yet she cannot delete this email any more than she can toss those blurry photographs, as if removing this evidence erases proof of his existence, their relationship. Sometimes she'll scan the photograph, save the document in a special file, thinking to create some meaningful photo storybook as a gift for his daughters.

Today, she finds no energy for such plans. Today, she clicks the little X to close the document. Today, she stares at the empty inbox and understands he will not write to her again.

# When a tourist asks on Facebook

Elizabeth Robin

*After We* ♥ *Hilton Head*

*I saw an episode of Shark Week . . . Are there sharks at Coligny?*

In seconds, the sharks circle.

The island offers 581 answers and counting
a relentless barrage of crashes
into the shark cage, *bon mot* nods
to class
  *Not on Hilton Head. Too expensive. They go to Myrtle*
*Beach.*
and country
  *They passed a law banning sharks.*
education
  *Another No Child Left Behind testimonial.*
and science (accompanied by screenshot)
  *From the looks of the tracker app they are enroute!*
the danger of public access
  *At Coligny, yes. It's a public entrance.*
and the need for gates
  *Not at the private ones. They don't let sharks in.*

A can-you-top-this game:
trounce the driest wit and win.

Cross the border into demean
and you miss the game's objective
a fun-filled say and display

in the obvious: *It's the ocean, so yes.*
the emotional (also, locals can tell you, a song): *Sharks are our homies.*
the policy angle: *I don't think they discriminate.*
the technicality: *Not in the Plaza LMFAO*
and the promotional: *There are LAND SHARKS at Tiki Hut.*

Moments later, *Are the gators dangerous on HHI?*

One romp ends, another begins . . .

**Shark** | **Amaury Cruz**

# Under the Talbird Oak

Susan Diamond Riley

Sunlight bounced off the waters of Skull Creek, magnified by the reflection of flames leaping from the nearby shore. A hawk cried in the distance. The captain shielded his eyes with his hand and shouted to his crew.

"Hurry it up, men! We've got a long day afore us."

Their faces dark with soot and sweat, nine men ran from the burning building and joined their leader on the marshy shoreline.

"How far to the next one?" a boy who couldn't have been more than fifteen asked, grinning from ear to ear.

"Less than a quarter hour by water, I suspect," Captain Martinangele replied.

His men climbed into the wooden boats they'd left and pulled onto the pluff mud on the creek's edge. Talking excitedly among themselves, they pushed off toward their next target.

"Quiet!" Martinangele told them in a loud whisper. "Do you want them to know we're coming?"

A hush fell over the crew as they rowed through the salty waters of Skull Creek. It was a misleading name for such a grand stretch of water, a wide river in most places, opening to massive bays on either end. In centuries to come it would be called the Intracoastal Waterway, separating the island of Hilton Head from the South Carolina mainland. On this balmy October morning in 1781, though, the waterway was a barrier between the wilderness of the Carolina colony and the bridgeless island. The island itself, the target of today's effort, was home to a couple of dozen plantation owners and the slaves who kept their fields of cotton, rice, and indigo profitable.

*Not for long,* Martinangele thought. *This island has picked the wrong side of this war.*

Ever confident in the power of their faraway King George, Philip Martinangele and the rest of the planters on neighboring Dawfuskie Island had naturally sided with the crown in this so-called "War of American Independence." What were these Hilton Head folks thinking declaring themselves "Patriots"? Traitors is what they were. And now their ill-thought choice had made enemies of these once-peaceful islands.

*Fools, the lot of them,* Martinangele thought, shaking his head. *They've brought all of this on themselves.* He'd received his orders earlier that week from further north. He was to take his Dawfuskie Island Royal Militia across Calibogue Sound and up Skull Creek, burning each plantation house to the ground as they came to it. As the mid-morning sun rose above the palmettos and live oaks lining the shore, they'd already destroyed three homes and a few out-buildings that the boys had torched just from excitement. Although that hadn't been part of the original orders, Martinangele figured the powers-that-be might appreciate the extra effort.

For the most part, he had ignored the wailing of the women as they watched their homes and a lifetime of belongings rendered to ashes. He'd not allowed his crew to hurt the women in any way, after all. With their own men off fighting their futile cause further north, the women had been left unprotected. They should be glad of Martinangele's lenience.

"Head ashore and light your torches," the captain told his men as they slid their boats through the marsh grass and onto the slick mud. Crabs scuttled frantically aside as the Royal Militia stomped toward the next fated house along their path.

Five miles ahead of the militia, Mary Ann Talbird lowered herself gingerly into a wooden rocking chair on the front porch of her home. It was only a bit past noon, and yet she felt the exhaustion of a full day. With her husband imprisoned on a British ship in Charleston Harbor, she'd had to take over management of their plantation in recent months. She sighed. *I don't blame John for doing his duty as a Patriot, but I sure wish he hadn't done it just now.* He was going to miss the birth of their first child, after all, and how was she going to run things all alone once the baby came?

Of course, she wasn't alone at all. The Talbirds owned two dozen souls who worked the fields for them and performed nearly all the household tasks. Mary Ann considered some of them almost like family and, although they never said so, she imagined they must feel the same about her. *Even so,* she thought, as she felt a swift kick inside her abdomen, *I sure wish John was here.*

"Miz Talbird, Miz Talbird!" Cassius burst from a line of palmetto shrubs and ran toward the house, his tiny arms and legs pumping.

Mary Ann strained to lean forward in her chair. "My goodness! What is it, child? Is someone hurt?"

The boy stopped at the foot of the steps, panting. "The Tories is coming, Miz Talbird! They's burning houses all up the creek! Josiah over at Cotton Hope tell me they just a few miles from here and headed this way!" Cassius plopped onto the bottom step and wiped his brow, beads of sweat dripping from his dark curls.

Mary Ann had pulled herself to standing and clung to the porch rail. "How many men are there, Cassius?"

"Josiah say they's near a dozen. They's travelin' up the creek in boats."

"Are people getting hurt?" She sickened at the thought of the friends she knew at those plantations—women whose husbands were also away fighting for independence.

Cassius shook his head. "I don't think so. They's just burnin' ever'thing and then headin' back to the water to get to the next one."

Drawn by the commotion, several other slaves gathered on and around the porch.

"What should we do, Miz Talbird?" asked an elderly man still clutching a sickle in his hand from his fieldwork. "We's a pretty sadly militia right here." He motioned to the ragtag group of men, women, and children. "I don't suppose we could fight 'em off."

Mary Ann shook her head. "No, Lucas, I don't suppose you could, and I'm surely in no condition to try." She instinctively clutched her belly and silently prayed. *Lord, show us mercy today.*

"Miz Talbird? We likely need to act quick," Lucas reminded her. "They could be here any time."

*Clear your head and think,* the young woman chided herself. She pressed at the dull ache in her back and tried to focus. *They're going to destroy everything I have. Everything that John and I have worked so hard for. Except....*

"All of you! Gather the others as fast as you can," she told her slaves in a rush. "Run inland into the woods. Hide yourselves, and don't come back until after you're sure they've already gone."

"But what about you, Miz Talbird?" Lucas asked. "You can't face them Tories all alone."

"Don't you worry about me. Surely, they wouldn't hurt a woman in my condition, don't you think?"

Lucas frowned. "Jes' in case, you sure you won't come hide with us, Miz Talbird?"

She waved him away with a shaky laugh. "You go on, now, the lot of you. And hurry!"

Obeying their mistress, the slaves turned and ran away from the house, past an enormous live oak, and into a dense thicket of trees and palmettos. Once they were out of sight, Mary Ann sighed heavily, clutched her belly, and once again lowered herself into her favorite rocking chair.

With each home burned, the Dawfuskie Royal Militia grew

more animated, more energized, wilder. Martinangele could see it in their eyes. After hours of intense rowing and the physical labor and pounding heat of igniting their former friends' homes, he'd expected the men might grow weary. Instead, the opposite had happened. They cheered, slapped each other on the back, and roared with laughter each time they returned to their beached boats on the shores of Skull Creek. The destruction was empowering, and any trepidation they may have felt that dawn as they paddled across Calibogue Sound toward Hilton Head Island was now clearly gone.

*Strange, too,* Martinangele thought, *that a couple of years ago we would never have dreamed of harming these people or their homes.* In fact, in prior years he'd come to parties at more than one of the houses they'd just destroyed and knew some of his men had, too. He'd thought those Hilton Head families were fine folk. Who would have thought they'd turn out to be traitors to the king? *Funny how war points out the true nature of people,* he thought.

By the time the band of men pulled up to the next house, Martinangele had lost count. Each marshy shore and tended yard space had begun to appear just as the others. How many plantations had they ruined today? Five? Seven? Either way, his superiors in the British Army would be pleased. It was late afternoon and dusk came early in the autumn, so perhaps this next attack would have to be the last. They'd make it a powerful one.

Once again, the Royalists dragged their boats up onto the pluff mud, their feet sinking in places as they stomped toward shore. Once on solid ground, they lit their torches and raced inland with a war cry.

But then Philip Martinangele's voice drowned out their own. "Stop! Stop at once!"

Confused, the men turned and stared at their captain, but then swiveled back towards the house ahead of them when they heard a woman's calm greeting.

"Good afternoon, brother." Mary Ann stood at the top of the porch stairs, her hands resting on her rounded belly. Her steady tone nearly concealed the anxiety she felt in saying them.

Martinangele cleared his throat. "Sister," he said, with a nod. Why hadn't he realized sooner that this was his militia's destination? True, he had not visited his sister-in-law's home on Hilton Head for several years. He had last seen her the previous winter when she had come to Dawfuskie to aid his wife—her own dear sister—in recovering from a fever. Of course, he had known that the task laid before him today would entail destroying the properties of folks he knew, but in his enthusiasm to serve the crown, he had chosen to ignore the possibility of hurting his own family. His was a mission to defeat the traitors. Would his wife understand that her youngest sister was the enemy?

Slowly, the pregnant woman descended the stairs, her hand gripping the railing as she neared the bottom. On the last step, she paused and grimaced, her free hand pressing the small of her back. Then, she took a deep breath and proceeded to walk toward her brother-in-law.

"How kind of you to check on me, brother," she said with a tight smile. "But you and your friends have wasted a trip, as I need nothing from you. Please tell my sister that I am well when you return home." With this, she nodded a goodbye and folded her hands in front of her.

"As captain of the Dawfuskie Royal Militia, I am under orders to burn *all* of the plantation homes along Skull Creek," Martinangele told her. "I am sorry, sister, but this is not of my own doing."

"Oh, but it is, sir," she said. "These men serve you, do they not? You could simply tell them to return to their boats, and they would obey you. Isn't that right?"

What was the captain to do? How would his wife ever forgive him if he caused the destruction of everything her favorite sister owned, and right as she was expecting her first child? What kind of man ruined his own family? On the other hand, Martinangele had declared his loyalty to the king and crown and must obey his orders from on high lest he be branded a traitor as well. And he would lose the respect of his men forever if he yielded to the wishes of a woman. He must follow through with his orders, exactly as he had been sworn to do. A decision made, he turned to his awaiting men and their burning torches.

"We were ordered to burn every Patriot home along Skull Creek," he told them. "But our orders said nothing of the contents of those homes."

A murmur ran through the band of confused men, but he hushed them and continued with his directions. Within moments, torches were extinguished and the entire militia had entered the Talbird house.

Under an ancient live oak tree two hundred feet from her house, Mary Ann watched as the Tory invaders emptied the residence of furniture, housewares, clothing, and more. She stood silently as each item was carefully placed with her in the protection of the draping branches. Surrounded by all of the possessions she and her husband had spent a lifetime collecting, she stood silently as the enormous tree's tiny leaves mottled the flickering light of the relit torches.

With the house fully ablaze, Philip Martinangele nodded to his sister-in-law and led his men back to the waters of Skull Creek and their own homes on Dawfuskie Island.

Mary Ann eyed the salvaged belongings beneath the old oak. "At least I managed to save something. I haven't lost everything," she thought, as another precious pain struck her.

*(Note: On October 19, 1781, the morning after the attack on Skull Creek, Mary Ann Talbird gave birth to her first son, a boy later called "Yorktown Henry" since he was born on the exact day that General Cornwallis surrendered to George Washington at Yorktown, VA. In*

*retaliation for the plantation burnings, Philip Martinangele was murdered in his sleep in December of that year by members of the Hilton Head Patriot Militia—a group that would then go down in history as "the Bloody Legion." Within months, John Talbird was released from the British prison ship in Charleston Harbor and returned to his family. The famous Talbird Oak, beneath which Mary Ann and her possessions sought safety, can still be seen within the grounds of Hilton Head Plantation.)*

*Talbird Tree* | Lindsay Pettinicchi

# Defiance

James A. Mallory

Little Ruby Bridges
all of six years old
immortalized by Rockwell

She strode, head high, back straight
white dress, anklets, and shoes
into a school where she belonged
to curses, jeers, threats

Men with guns protect her,
restrain White mob
that 2-4-6-8
didn't want to integrate

Generational image
of courage,
defiance

Sixty years later,
Little Ruby Bridges—
young symbol of
quiet disobedience—
a flashpoint for those
looking to sanitize
America's troubled past

Defiance

It seems her life, as told
in a children's book
and a Disney film
may be too much
for some delicate minds

Ignorant adults and politicians fret
historic truth will burden
the young with the guilt
of those who tried to keep

Little Ruby Bridges
from defiantly walking
into a school where she belonged

# ALTERATIONS

*Parrish Mills Covered Bridge* | Steve Tate

# Ten Minutes

David Inserra

James Burke opened both eyes and inhaled the fresh Hilton Head Island air. Far across the freshly mown fairway near the third hole, his left eye saw a motionless figure standing amongst the shrubs. The man had long cheekbones, thin lips, pale skin, and spiked brown hair. This being the rainy season, it was no surprise that the man wore a long black rain slicker. On the Island, people often left their houses with rain gear to protect themselves against the pop-up storms that frequently tore across the land this time of the year.

As James thought the words *pop-up storms,* the images in his left eye began to change. Storm clouds sent creeping shadows across the grass. They intensified, twisted, rolled, and danced through the sky, barreling toward the distant figure. The stranger raised his arms to will away the approaching violence as the wind grabbed at his rain slicker.

The scene played out through James' left eye. Trees swayed. The sky blackened. Thunder shattered the island's calm. Surrounding shrubs thrashed at the man's body while a roaring wind echoed across the land. A flash of lightning blinded James, forcing him to shield his eyes. In that instant, the world fell quiet.

Then, sounds of nature returned.

Distant warblers gave their joyous calls.

Crickets and cicadas sang alongside the nearby lagoon.

Across the fairway, James' left eye saw the stranger, his motionless body sprawled across the ground. A shadow grew from the nothingness around the man. Tall and lean, the shade of something hideous expanded, its form writhing as it rose to ten feet. Engulfed in blackness, the figure had a waning crescent moon-shaped head. It leaned forward, hovering over the body on the ground. Rail-thin arms unfolded, reaching toward the still figure. Foot-long, dart-like bony fingers clicked and danced back and forth as if the darkness were waiting, deciding.

When James closed his right eye, the world became one. The dreadful creature hovering over the unconscious figure vanished.

"Looks like we might be in for a storm."

Gulping a mouth full of air, James spun. Less than five feet away, the clear, undoubled image of a man stood. He wore a long black rain slicker. He had long cheekbones, thin lips, pale skin, and spiked brown hair, just like the man across the fairway.

"I ... I guess ..." James muttered, turning back. His left eye still saw the dark figure hovering over the collapsed form on the grass.

"You okay, buddy?"

A charge of lightning miles away lit up the island. Dark clouds kissed the edge of the horizon. James' respiration increased. His hands began to shake. James pushed past the man and hurriedly started along the cart path as he called, "Take cover. Take cover now."

It all began three years ago. James suffered a minor heart attack. After triple bypass surgery and the repair of an atrial septal defect, he began to experience double vision. The images in his left eye were at eleven o'clock. The images in his right eye were at five o'clock. He had 20/20 vision. It was just that his eyes weren't working together. At first, this proved just to be an annoyance. While walking down the street, he would see what appeared to be two separate cars, one on the road, closing in on his right and the other heading directly toward him. Over time, the troublesome double vision seemed to fade. But it was always there. His brain just got used to it. When he looked left, he got into the habit of closing one eye to experience single vision. He tipped his head when he drove, enabling his singular vision to return. Life went on like this for over two years. Then, the double vision got worse. This strain on his brain became mixed with a tingling sensation along the side of his head, like swarms of maggots scraping down his left cheek, over his gums, teeth, and nostrils, and digging deep into the corner of his eye. When a doctor ordered an MRI, they discovered a tumor living in a sensitive area of his head called Meckel's cave. This tumor exerted pressure on the cavernous sinus, the home of arteries and nerves that control the eyes and the face.

*A tumor.*

The doctors gave James three options. He could live with the tumor. He could have dangerous surgery, though no doctor would recommend this unless it were a matter of life or death. Or he could have Gamma Knife radiosurgery, where they would use radiation to try and kill the tumor.

James chose Gamma Knife.

A year after the procedure, the double vision remained, and the visions began. At times, James' left eye sometimes saw people and things that weren't visible in his right eye. It wasn't that the images in his left eye weren't there. They just weren't there yet. The turmoil in his brain had caused his left eye to see ten minutes into the future.

A week after his experience on the golf course, James stood by the mailboxes. In his left eye, his neighbor, Magda, cried—her long frame wrapped over the broken body of her child, Gabe. Moments earlier, James' left eye saw Gabe zipping through the parking lot on his motorized scooter. The work truck barreled into the development. Commotion, noise, destruction, and death followed. And there was the shadow. It hovered over Magda. Slipping to the left, its form rolling to the right, it writhed, waiting for an opening to take the child.

James closed his right eye. His vision became one. And he waited.

Soon, Gabe would ride his scooter through the lot. He knew it. It always worked that way. He could prevent this tragedy if he could delay Gabe from riding his scooter, stay focused, and keep an eye on the surroundings.

That's when he heard the buzz of the tiny engine.

Gabe zipped his scooter along the street. He took a sharp left into the lot.

James stepped into the open. He waved at the young boy. They were friends.

Gabe waved back.

James gestured for him to come closer.

The scooter turned.

At the same time, the work truck tore into the lot.

James swept forward, grabbing the boy.

The truck swerved as it clipped the scooter and sent it flying, crashing into the side of the clubhouse.

After this latest incident, James began wearing an eyepatch on his right eye to block the double images. He lost his stereo-optic vision, but at least he kept his sanity.

Approaching the red light at the intersection of Dillon Road and Highway 278, James tapped the brakes of his RAV4. On Saturday afternoons, Hilton Head's traffic always increased with the change-over from all of the surrounding resorts. When the car stopped, he checked the heavy oncoming traffic to his left. He blinked a few times while his white-knuckled hands gripped the steering wheel.

James closed his eyes, slipped off the patch, and lowered his head while waiting for the light to change. Leaning back, James rubbed his eyes while listening to the gentle purr of the engine.

When he turned back to the street, he heard a bang.

A body slammed against the side of the vehicle. Moments ago, she had been blonde. Now, her hair sizzled, crackling with flame. Through his left eye, he saw her face, smoldering, charred, and black as fire engulfed her from head to toe. Her hand pounded the window as terrified blue eyes pleaded for help. The wind pulled at her skin, peeling it away, causing it to float through the air, swirling on tiny tornados of energy.

A blurred figure passed by James' left eye. Someone dove on the woman, knocking her off of her feet, out of his field of vision.

Now, he saw the vehicles in front of the park, at the other side of the intersection. His left eye saw a mass of flaming metal where a blue Ford intertwined with a long, low-souped-up BMW. The palm tree vanity plate of the Ford melted to ash. People rushed through the street. Some screamed. Others cried. One man leaped out of a van with a sweatshirt wrapped around his arms. He ran to one of the vehicles, trying to pull its flaming door open to rescue someone inside. Fire and smoke pushed him back each time he closed in on his target.

Turmoil surged through the scene as the dark, shadowed figure expanded from nothingness along the side of the road. Its arms un-folded, reaching to see what it could scavenge from the destruction.

James turned away. He closed his eyes. Replacing his eyepatch, he returned to reality.

A moment later, something tapped the window.

"Hey, you got a problem, buddy?" the cop said loud enough to be heard inside the vehicle.

James didn't move.

"Okay, buddy." The cop pointed. "Pull over to the side of the road."

If James had just left, the cop would probably have come after him, thinking he was drinking or having an attack. If he pulled over, he could talk to the cop. Maybe he could convince him that things here were about to change.

James inched the vehicle to the side of the road and lowered his window.

"You were sitting there for some time, pal. Something going on?"

"No, sir."

"License and registration."

While sliding the documents to the officer, James checked the time on his dashboard. He needed to act. He couldn't see her face again. He couldn't see the destruction that would soon shatter the surrounding area.

The officer tapped the plastic card a few times with his index finger. "Mr. James Burke. What's with the eyepatch, James? You high?"

James shook his head. "I ... I have an issue with my eyes."

The cop waited.

"Officer," James noticed the nametag over the man's left breast. "Inserra. We ... We don't have much time."

"Excuse me?"

"Here." James pointed toward the intersection. "In less than ten minutes, this area's going to change."

"Change?"

"Yeah. But we can stop it. No one will get hurt."

The cop's eyes tightened. He gave a slow nod while taking a step back. "And who are you gonna hurt?"

"It's not me. I saw it."

The officer's hand hovered near his weapon. "So, go ahead. Tell me about it."

"It's just ..." James pulled the latch, and the door opened.

"Stay in the vehicle."

"Look." James hopped out. Taking a step toward the officer, he pointed past the park. "We need to stop the traffic. Just for a few minutes. That should do it."

The cop's weapon left its holster. "Get back in the vehicle."

James bit his bottom lip. His wide eyes jumped left and right. His head jittered. His hands shook. "You don't understand," he pleaded.

"I sure do, you high piece of shit."

"There's a woman. She's in a blue Ford. She has a palm tree vanity plate." He pointed frantically to the street. "Someone heading west is going to lose control of their vehicle. It's going to cross the median, and they're going to have a head-on. The woman ... she's ... she's gonna burn if we don't do something. People are going to die."

"You're gonna die if you don't get back into your vehicle."

James jumped forward, knocking the officer's arm aside. He charged into the street toward the intersection. Horns sounded. Vehicles swerved. People panicked to get around the crazy man running through traffic. James kept low as he dodged around one vehicle after another, hoping that the cop wouldn't fire into the crowd.

Reaching 278, James scanned both directions of the highway.

It was going to happen. He knew it.

Then he saw the Ford with the palm tree vanity plate. The vehicle headed east toward him and her unknown destiny. James leaped into the street. He threw his arms in the air. He had to flag her down. He had to get her to stop. Someone would be coming west along the road at any moment. This other vehicle would cause the destruction. This other vehicle would bring about her death.

The driver of the Ford cut the wheel and skidded.

A sports car swerved as it buzzed by.

Another car slammed on its brakes, sideswiping a pickup truck.

A work van bounced left and right, its brakes sending clouds of smoke into the air.

Heading eastbound, a BMW crossed the median. It careened into the westbound lane.

The bumper of the BMW caught James' legs and threw him in the air. His head snapped back, smashing into the windshield. His body tumbled up the front of the vehicle, over the roof, into the air, rolling like a rag doll, drifting along the wind.

The BMW skidded across the road, shot over the bike path, through the grass, shattering a rail fence as it smashed into a deep gully outlining the park.

At James' side, something unfolded.

A dark figure, long, lean, and shadowed, flew with him until he crashed.

∂❧

He opened his eyes.

A blonde woman sat in the chair next to his bed.

She smiled. She held his hand. "I'm Ellen."

Both of his eyes blinked at her single image. A single vase of flowers rested on the overbed table along the side of the room, and a single massive oak swayed in the breeze outside his window. When he closed his right eye, the images didn't change.

The woman beside him had exquisite blue eyes and round, bright cheeks. She smiled and tilted her head to one side, causing her blonde hair to sweep loosely across her shoulders. Her long blue dress, with a colorful floral design, accented her well-defined figure.

He knew her face. The most beautiful face he had ever seen.

"I wanted to thank you for what you did." She averted her eyes.

He saw this woman touched by pain and flame.

He saw her dying.

Then he saw her hovering over him. She held him close, urging life to remain in his body.

He turned to the light shining in through the window. The warmth of the sunshine caused him to lean deep into the pillows. "I ... I remember," his raspy voice cracked.

"Don't try to speak. Tubes and machines have kept you alive these past months. You're doing okay now."

He shook his head. "You helped me? You came to me when I was dying?"

She nodded. "And you helped me. The officer told me what you did."

Neither of them could take their eyes off of each other.

"You must think I'm crazy," James breathed.

She touched his cheek, then leaned close. In a whisper, she said, "I believe you."

# lip service

Kyle Zubatsky

red lipstick

seducer of hapless men
powerful
bold
shocks
mocks
defiant
self-reliant
scarlet harlot
tempter
trickster
cast a spell
burned at the stake
no mistake
a Jezebel's fall from grace
shame on her face

Marilyn's personal shade Rouge Diabolique
five coats she applied
lied about red algae
blood mud and fish scales
old cosmetic fails
we've come a long way from 5000 BC

pardon Elizabeth Arden
tubes of ruby

passed along the Ave
suffragettes to have
their lips proclaim
name
tame
blame
misogynist men

Hitler hated sanguine shrews
pouty lips
plump hips
sway
pray
for a hallelujah hit
intimidation
emasculation
Aryan purity
his insecurity

WWII images burned
Rosie the Riveter
arm curled
no ordinary girl
lips tinted garnet
we can do it
military kits issued
a tube of cherry
to fight
an adversary
hypnotic
patriotic

Kyle Zubatsky

red lipstick

harmless grease
or sexual release
superhero
or super villain

# I Walked the Line

Denise K. Spencer

One day after school, I came home to find Dad arguing heatedly with someone on the telephone. Embarrassment and apprehension rose from my stomach to my throat when I realized it was Mr. Johnson, the driver's education teacher, who was receiving Dad's vitriol. Unfortunately, it was only a matter of time before this disagreement over course requirements would appear from behind the curtain, and I knew it. My permission slip might not be signed.

Mr. Johnson's position was immovable; all new automobiles were required to be outfitted with lap belts for the first time in 1968. My school district and its insurance company made it compulsory that the belts be worn in driver's training, so my teacher's job required both his, and my, compliance.

My father was a funeral director. His hearse, with landau panels removed and a flashing light affixed to the top, doubled as an ambulance. Dad was trained in first aid and was called to the scene of many accidents. His experience with both hearse and ambulance led him to believe, with all of his heart, that it was safer to be without a seatbelt than with one. He trusted his own eyes that people thrown from vehicles had a better survival rate than those trapped inside or severed by the belt itself. He may have been right, as those early lap belts were not well designed. And at the time, seatbelts were not yet mandated to be worn by all drivers on the roads in Michigan. So, he declined to allow me to wear one in driver's training, or at any other time for that matter.

Often in life, one has to walk a fine line. It might be walking the line between getting enough sleep or meeting a deadline. It might involve deciding how to manage between maintaining a bank balance and paying off creditors. Or drinking enough to be social without incurring a stagger.

In my junior year of high school (1968-69), I had to navigate the line between my father and my driver's education teacher. For 17-year-old me, nothing was more important. My license, and permission to use it, hung in the balance.

If I didn't play by the school's rules *and* by my dad's rules, I might not drive until my shoulder-length flip with straight bangs was framed by gray tendrils. I lied to my father for the first time I can remember. He trusted me without question. I ached down to my toes as I told him I was granted an exception and not required to wear the seatbelt in class, but my teacher could not put it in writing lest he lose his job. The truth was that I wore the belt each and every time I got in the training vehicle. But as the course neared completion, I feared I was about to get caught.

For the driving test, I was required to wear the belt or I would lose four points on the exam—the maximum I could lose and still pass. And of course, Dad would see the results, including the score. If I didn't lose at least four points, my father would never allow me to drive, even if I earned my license. That much was painfully clear. And a loss of even one more point meant I'd not earn the license anyway.

Testing day arrived and, shaking, I dropped into the driver's seat. Mr. Johnson, equipped with a clipboard, fastened his belt and said I could start when I was ready. I looked at him and he looked at me, saying nothing more. I sighed, turned the key in the ignition, and with my belt's two halves lying flaccid on the bench seat, inched forward.

Terror rode shotgun; not terror of the road, but terror of making a mistake. Would I forget to use the blinker? Misjudge the timing between light changes at the traffic signal? Park too far from the curb? Oh, dear. I feared I might vomit before I got to the next block.

Returning to the school parking lot, I turned off the car, still shaking, and I looked with hope into the eyes of Mr. Johnson. His glare frightened me—but quickly it turned into a smile. I was never so happy to lose precisely four points on an examination in all my life!

I had walked the line.

# High Anxiety

Judy Bauer

It's early at the café.
The eastern sun
illuminates patterns on our table
in stripes and splotches.
Steam from my coffee rises,
while across from me
he shifts in his chair.
I remember his childhood,
the scent of grass and dust in his hair.

Phrases flow between us
flecked with words like computer,
dorm, roommate, classes.
The nearby geranium droops.
It hasn't been watered
for some time.

I search his brow, the hollow of his cheek,
to see if what he needs is in him now.
We say goodbye and he is gone,
like the mist over a lake
that burns off and disappears.

Outside, workmen with pneumatic drills
break a sidewalk into pieces.
Later, when the surface is repaired
no one will know it was ever broken.

What I am feeling is high anxiety,
as when the river floods
and leaves a gap in the shoreline
which used to hold flowers and trees.
Even headstones.
A landscape that will never be the same.

# My Mother Ate a Mail Truck

Miho Kinnas

It's four o'clock. My beautiful mother heads for the mailbox. The mailman hops out of the truck. He hands her a package. I leave the window in the den and open the door for her armful. There is no mother. There is no mailman. I run out and look down the straight road. No sign of a mail truck or mother. They have disappeared into thin air, but two plump envelopes are inside the mailbox. I didn't hear the bang of the flap or the distinct engine noise. I sigh. *My mother. Yet again.*

It's four o'clock. The neighborhood comes alive. Neighbors on my left toddle toward the mailbox. Neighbors on my right find their mailbox empty. Not even junk. I whisper to the friendliest of them that my mother has gone missing, but the neighbor simply winces as if having a toothache.

"Well, dear, don't worry. Your beautiful mother will turn up before you know it. Nothing happens in this community. By the way, how's college?" She turns around without waiting for my reply.

The retired football coach raises his voice. "It is four o'clock. How come house 13 received the mail but not us? House 17 doesn't have any mail either. What is going on?" He keeps looking inside the mailbox.

The skinny woman and her short next-door neighbor from the cul-de-sac begin conversing with their eyes occasionally glancing at me. Two crows fly straight up to the top of the live oak.

A car is coming. Dad's Honda. He slows and rolls down the window and mouths hello to nobody and everybody. People raise the corner of their lips and a hand halfway. He turns into the driveway and then the garage. He steps out of the car, and the car beeps twice. He listens to what I say and says, "So, she took off with the mailman? Is that what you are saying?" He snatches the two envelopes away from my hand and bangs the door. I probably must fix him something to eat.

The short neighbor is speaking to be heard. "Well, I was expecting a letter from my sister. We need to call the post office. But it is no use. You know they won't pick up the phone. Will someone go to the post office tomorrow?"

The skinny woman tells me in an icy voice, "Ask your mother what she did with the mailman and our mail when she comes home. Will you?"

*Yes, if she ever comes home.*

# A Stranger in the Parlor of Death

David Rosenberg

I sat in the parlor of death,
strangely detached,
as the Rabbi intoned his nasal cadence
for the man he did not know.

The young daughter, in sheer blouse and nail polish,
could not follow his thread
as it shuttled between beauty and inanity
concerning the man she could not have known.

The ex-wife, sobbing, sniffing, sighing,
would not hear
his efforts to weave sanctity and purpose
into the life of the man she had long given up knowing.

The sister, stolid caretaker, stunned mourner,
strained to eke meaning from
his tapestry of truths and authorities
about the man she had known too briefly.

And my detachment slowly transformed into grief.
The Rabbi's words could not alter the facts.
A life was lost meaninglessly, needlessly, beyond our ability
to reach the man we could no longer know.

# Rust

Bill Newby

Among my peers,
we joke about forgetfulness.

But it's not funny
being unable to recall
a name, a face, good restaurants,
which story others have already heard.

My father had several favorite tales.

How he helped the milkman at dawn
as horses pulled the wagon.

The choice his coach offered:
"Cigarettes or track!"

Starting in the mailroom.
Finishing as V. P.

Each story precious,
even on the hundredth telling,
and often sparking a true laugh
or fresh "Wonderful!"

Stories that cradled the past
and helped to keep us close.

But I don't want to write poems
that lack freshness and punch—
the same stuff, over and again.

If my past disappears,
will the present be enough?

# The Small Man with Grotesque Feet

Eric Johnson

He walked through the church parking lot, hidden from the morning sun by a ball cap that slid over his eyes, the brim resting on the bridge of his nose. His gray jacket hung to his knees, and the hem of his white T-shirt drooped below the bottom of his jacket. Adults were preparing for a Halloween trunk-or-treat, making it plausible that the small man lurching through the lot could be mistaken for a boy masquerading in his father's clothing.

Children from neighboring public housing were lured by the bouncy house that blossomed in the middle of the lot and the white tent offering video gaming stations. They stopped hopefully at the open hatches of vehicles parked along the perimeter, waiting for invitations to "Take what you want" and then digging into the horde of candy and sugar-laden drinks piled inside each trunk. The small man ignored the candy and avoided the gaming stations where teenagers sat killing animated zombies. He took no notice of the fried fish being flipped in a kettle of oil or the succulent Boston butts smoking on the grill. He treaded toward the far corner of the lot where boots, brogans, sneakers, slippers, and slides were displayed under a red-lettered banner proclaiming "FREE SHOES."

His hands were stuffed into the pockets of his jacket, causing his shoulders to roll forward as though he were a tiny workman pulling a heavy wagon. His feet made a rhythmic clip-clop that no one could hear over the drone of generators, squeals of excited children, and occasional hoots of adults gorging themselves on smoked pork and fried fish.

Nor did anyone notice that the small man wore no shoes. People might have observed, were it not for the distractions, the man's feet were actually blocks of peeling skin, mounds of dead, mud-colored flesh, spotted with open sores the size of quarters, streaked with festering fissures that oozed stinking fluid and microscopic parasites. It would be insufficient to describe the man's feet as unnatural; they were inhuman, perhaps other-worldly. The toes on each foot had melded together into hooked claws, twin curved sabers revealing the menace of a raptor's beak. A sharp bone pierced the heel of each foot, exposing bleached three-inch spear tips.

A boy dressed in a cheap, baggy Spider Man costume pointed at what sprouted from the small man's ankles and yelled, "Yo! Where you get them fake monster feet?" His mother pulled him away. Anything that hideous had to be expensive, and she wasn't having it.

The small man approached the footwear table, taking time to fondle and sniff several shoes. An elderly woman sat on a folding chair well-placed to assist shoppers, which ensured no one took more than one pair. "Can I help you, young man?" she asked, even though she couldn't tell if he were young or old.

The small man lifted a pair of size-five ladies walking shoes. They had a label on the tongue that proclaimed the shoe's brand, The Queen.

"Ahh, I see you've picked The Queen sneak," said the woman. "That's a good sneak, but those are for women. Plus, you ain't getting your feet into that shoe. You need a size ...." She blanched at the smell of rotting flesh that rose from the ground on which the man stood. She had seen some crusty things in her day but nothing like the monstrosities at the bottom of this man's legs. She had no idea what size shoe he wore or if such a size existed. "Child," she said looking up at him as he examined The Queen, "what you done to your feet?"

The small man pointed to the banner, and the woman relented.

"Okay, baby. You can take the shoes, but I don't know what you think you're gonna do with them."

The small man clopped his way across the street toward a miniature figure standing alone in a doorway. Her height was that of a three- or four-year-old, but her face visible inside a pink hooded sweatshirt revealed a womanly countenance of maturity and wisdom. She wore baggy jeans, and her feet were shrouded inside black plastic bags. The small man bowed slightly before he got onto one knee and held the shoes toward her as though making an offering or supplication. She extended one slender hand toward the gift, which she grasped while pressing the palm of her other hand against her chest. With his head slightly bowed, the man returned the gesture. She tilted her head, exposing a smile, and extended her hand toward his ailing feet. In that moment, their bodies shared an incandescent glow and the once-festering feet flashed a blue-green aura that dissipated almost as quickly as it appeared. The natural light exposed the man's slender toes, sculptured heels, and curved arches, all encased beneath the smooth texture of tawny flesh.

# REBUILDING

*Old Sheldon Church* | Tom Moseley

# The Toolbox

Suzie Eisinger

The package was sitting on her doorstep when she arrived home
that night. Twenty inches wide and surprisingly heavy, it was wrapped
in brown paper and addressed with a feminine script. Claire frowned
at the return address—it was her father's home.

The father she had buried two months ago.

Claire shook her head slowly, the tip of her mousy ponytail
glancing the back of her neck. Her purse and jacket now lay in a
forgotten heap on the floor as she placed the package on the counter
for a closer look. She pulled at the tape, and the heavy paper fell
away, revealing a shock of fire-engine red.

Her father's toolbox—part of his life for as long as he had been
part of hers. Dented and worn down to the gray metal in those spots
where his hands touched most, the inside was a picture of order.
Compartments wiped clean of dust and housing an array of tools
of every size and function, this toolbox was her father's pride and
joy. Every time a neighbor or friend needed help with their car, a
rusty hinge, a faucet that wouldn't stop dripping, her father headed
to the garage for his box and was on his way. No questions asked.

Claire swept a hand across the tools, a flood of memories surfac-
ing with each contact. A late-in-life daughter for a man knowing
little of women except the one he'd loved and lost too soon, Claire
navigated with ease the world of three-dimensional objects, how
they fit together, how they were mended. Theirs was a world of few
words whenever they worked in the garage, the oldies radio station
providing a soundtrack as they made something whole together.
She pulled up a sleeve as she continued her explorations, revealing a
hand-shaped bruise in its colorful last stages of healing, only a little
sore now. Sadly, he hadn't been able to teach her how to navigate

the world of humans, to understand what was healthy and what was over the line. That not everyone could be trusted.

She'd met her husband at the small-town general store where she'd worked throughout and after high school. From the moment he casually tossed his credit card onto the counter, she'd been captivated, his entitled air of confidence sweeping into her world and carrying her away. Her father, initially pleased with the idea that his daughter would be so well-cared-for by this man, offered little resistance to the match. Within the year, she was inhabiting a new home, a new life, a new identity different from anything she'd known in her previous twenty years.

Perhaps she was to blame, Claire told herself—she hadn't adapted fast enough to the lifestyle, the standards, the expectations necessary for living in his world. Claire reached down and pulled at a stray thread on her blouse, brushed away an invisible speck of lint. She glanced at her manicure, a perfect glossy red, blemished by cuticles bitten absently when no one was looking.

She checked her watch. She would clear the packaging away before he came home. The idea of a toolbox would be amusing to him at best, insulting at worst. His wife didn't need a toolbox. They hired help when repairs were needed. She never told him of the hours spent learning by her father's side.

A sealed envelope lay beneath the metal tray, her name in the same cursive handwriting as on the packaging. It was not her father's writing—she'd know his strong slanted strokes anywhere. This was her aunt's writing, her father's spinster sister who tried her best to bridge the gap between widowed father and daughter emerging into a bewildering world of adolescence.

*These belong to you now. Never forget who you are. Love, Dad.*

Claire stared at the note. The simple words were his, she knew. But when had he dictated them? She then opened a folded document inside, notarized and official looking. The deed to their house. Her house now. Her fingers glanced over the raised seal of the document—officiated over a year before.

She closed her eyes and exhaled slowly, letting go of the breath she'd held quietly for years.

The next morning, Claire left, the toolbox in one hand and in the other a small suitcase containing only what she'd brought with her five years before. To anyone watching, she looked no different. But to Claire, she stood a little taller, her stride was longer, her diminished strength was returning. Her father's daughter was going home where she belonged.

*Toolbox* | **Cathy Bateman**

# Everywhere

Barry Dickson

"Where are you going, dear?" she called from upstairs.
"Out looking for a poem. I'll be back at dinnertime. Bye."

I will find one in the park for sure.
It might land on a branch.
Or bend my way in a breeze.
Or poke its little head up through the ground.
Once I found a poem in the park pond
making tiny bubbles with its lips.
"Look," I said to my friend Freddie, "a poem."
"What are you talking about," he said,
"it's a damn fish."  Good guy, that Freddie;
not so good at seeing poems.

If I don't find one in the park
I'll be surprised, but not discouraged.
There are plenty on the streets--
under cars, in skimpy skirts,
they even sleep in doorways.
Arnold once found a beauty on a beach.
Whitman on a little promontory.
Keats on an urn. Byron in darkness.
Wow, an eye so sharp
you could spot a poem in the dark.

Most poems are dying to be found.
They call to you from everywhere.
Train wheels. Bell peals. Pounding hearts.
Frost found several in the snow.
(A guy named Frost finding poems in the snow
is in itself a little poem, don't you think?)
Byron even heard one call from inside Anne
not to mention Florence, Harriet, Caroline, Marion and Mary.
Apparently it's true, women love a man who listens.

So what then is the population of these poems,
there being no census for such things?
Some say they are countless billions. A poem in every
flake and bird and kiss and blade
and branch and wing and rose and nose and leaf
and child and flea and field and tear and soul and heart.

But there is yet another school, calling poems extremely rare.
You must search long and wander miles for weeks
or months to find just one, they say. And even then
they often are imposters, like fool's gold.
They claim there have been maybe a few thousand ever, tops.
Tough crowd.

I favor the former. But perhaps the latter have a point
because I found no poem that day—how odd.
Last week, I found one in the glove compartment.
I don't know how long it had been in there,
or why I never noticed it—between the unpaid parking tickets,
the expired insurance card, and the empty space
where the registration should have been.
I called it "Negligence: An Ode."

That evening, as promised, I did return at dinnertime.
We went to Jean Jacque's Bistro, our favorite local spot,
where I had, of course, my favorite local soup.
But tonight...I noticed something I had never seen before.
One crouton, a large grayish one, seemed to meander,
as though rudderless. Whilst a smaller one floated
directly for it, I suspect deliberately.
The big one, I thought, it's the Bismarck.
The small one, H.M.S. Hood. I gasped.
"What's the matter?" said my girlfriend.
I turned to the kitchen and called out:
"Waiter! There's a poem in my soup!"

# Soot

Diane Valeri

Through the hazy, neon air
I sip my morning coffee
scanning the iridescent pink and orange waves.
A film of soot covers my white table,
                    a layer of black ash.
The weatherman says
our technicolor dawn
is a product of a half million
California Redwoods and Sequoias
                    incinerated in a raging wildfire.
While I enjoy my flip-flop summer
eating bagels under my red umbrella,
these once-rooted, ancient ladies
flew 3,000 miles on the wings of a jet stream,
cross-country, nine miles high,
landing here
                    to visit their Carolina cousins.
I recall measuring the girth of one Redwood
last summer in San Francisco.
Four sets of arms
                    couldn't circle her broad trunk.
I spray and wipe
the dusty residue on my chairs,
the lifeless debris of
once vibrant, once green,
once oxygen-producing leaves
                    of graceful centurions.

A deadly atmospheric shadow
hovers on our shoreline
punctuating the grief.

                    Ashes to ashes. Dust to dust.

The nutrient-rich carbon
returns to the soil
to grow another tree

                    on our side of the continent.

What a meager tribute

                    to the tall, proud ladies of the West

# Crumbling Infrastructure

### Elizabeth Robin

My life runs a constant newsreel in my mind and lands now on a particular bread-and-butter shot, the precision topspin backhand down the line that won so many matches. Within an inch of the corner, every time. My opponents would think early on *No way she can keep making that shot!* and so continue to feed balls right into my deadly wheelhouse. Effortless, that turn, shoulder to the net post, right arm muscles rippling as I push powerful hips into and through the ball, swing easily out, a puff of airy tendon, focused so cleanly on the target I feel I can see each fiber protruding from its rubbery outer coating. Then, ready, a light jouncing from the balls of my feet, weapon comfortably in hand, already back to the middle, a slim and supple counterpunching machine facing the next challenge. The smug satisfaction each time the ball strikes that precise six-square-inch space in the opponent's court never wavers.

"Ha!" slips out often at the standstill, arms akimbo posture, the disappointment shown across the net. More so if that opponent tries to run it down, flailing helplessly, racquet never reaching within a yard of its target. I earn every flexed muscle, every easy breath, every skilled swing in hundreds of weight reps, miles of running, thousands of practice balls. A body, fueled by the healthiest of diets, senses it can transcend any obstacle, push past any human limit.

But now, "Ha!" escapes my lips for an entirely different reason. The series of movements the doctor's assessment requires, that same shoulder turn, that jouncing, prompt autonomic gasp, pain scraping away my game face in an instant. "Spinal stenosis," he says. "Physical therapy can help," he adds.

As I listen to a doctor younger than my son detail bone structures, pointing diligently to each respective part as he talks, I wonder how someone so devoted to healthy habits falls into such disrepair. As if regular investments had not been made on its maintenance. Fresh fruits and vegetables, packed with antioxidants. Thirty-plus minutes of aerobics attended to more religiously than a good Catholic on holy days takes communion. A strong core, endurance running, strength training. And yet, it seems each decade some other youngster prods and peers via the latest machinery and reveals some new level of deterioration.

The elbow failed first, then this foot and that tendon and this knee. Now, my spine. It seems my spirit houses in a crumbling infrastructure without the tax base to restore it to effective transportation. Some sort of pothole, it seems, has dug out a spot where a little pavement slipped sideways. The macadam itself, crusted from a rough winter, allows little flexibility. When inclement weather crackles, it threatens to disintegrate even more dramatically.

Where has my real self gone? The one I remember with tantalizing tactility, a holographic film with sensory imaging. Youthful energy, sense of power, gone. And that perfect backhand? I have not executed it once in the last twenty years. The feeling I could run miles longer slowed to a walk in the last ten. Each time I try to resurrect who I was, this body betrays me. Life has become a war of attrition. A story of diminishment. A capitulation in pill form.

This change has not been a surprise. Even at 20 I knew one juke the wrong way might mean an injury that ends some athletic venture. How many friends never got to play in college or the pros? Older friends often regaled me with their latest twinge, tweak, loss of movement. I've watched their hip replacements, swimming-pool therapies, artificial knees. Bionic is the new 60.

What puzzles, what I never expected? That memory. The mental acuity did not suffer an equal blunting from years of use. In most arenas, a great blessing. But on a tennis court? Even though I cannot push off my right foot, sprint up, scoop and dump a slice-away dropshot just over the net, I can still feel myself doing it. Every movement, every strategy percolates within that newsreel in my head. The body has frayed about the edges, but the years have not sanded down the map of memories, not blurred them to some fuzzy imitation that softens the blow of what's lost. This realization brings both wonder and frustration.

The young doctor tells me I'm lucky, smart to have spent my life staying fit and active. That physicality promises more years enjoying dog walks and beach days. Those not like me, he says, soon lose the ability to move at all. Joy is found when a set of arduous exercises, what years ago I would have called warm-up stretches, might rebuild and maintain the status quo. Triumphs are measured in pain management and alternate activities. Championships arrive by resuming long walks, a holiday hike, a cross-country ski run, or tubing down a lazy river. Any tax is worth such a trophy.

# Understand the Assignment

Denise K. Spencer

Be ejected
from the soft place.

Absorb love.
Grow confidence.
Gather values, skills,
friends and lovers.

Play hard.
Work hard.
Love hard.
Fall hard.

Become hard--
then discard hard.
Remember the soft place.

Teach the young ones.
Reach the young ones.
Be there
as long as they need.

Play by the rules.
Use all the tools.
Fish where the fish are.
Plan for your memoir.

Connect the dots,
and be grateful.
Do all the good you can,
for as long as you can.

Refuse to wear out.
But when you do,
pass the baton.

# Alive Enough

Jim Riggs

Am I ever
alive enough
without spring flowers
everywhere underfoot?

Am I ever
alive enough
without a multitude
of multicolored birds?

Am I ever
alive enough
without massive mammals
living in my forest
and in my ocean?

Am I ever
alive enough
without migratory waterfowl
swimming into and flying out of my pond?

# The Navajo Doctor

Marty Ferris

At four a.m. on a Thursday morning, William Hilton Parkway was almost deserted. A blue Plymouth's headlights pierced the darkness while crisp, fall breezes flooded through its open windows. Twenty minutes later, the thin, six-foot tall driver, sixty-five-year-old cardiac surgeon Thomas Meadows, swung into a side road, slowed down, and stopped at the staff parking entrance of Hilton Head Regional Medical Center.

"Good morning, Doc," called out parking attendant Jeff Goodwin, who cheerfully waved him in as he had done each weekday morning for the past twelve years. Thomas Meadows smiled at the middle-aged black man and drove through the gates. The facial muscle lines around the doctor's mouth briefly deepened as he thought about how these early hour pleasantries and his frequent weekend fishing trips with Jeff and his children would soon be just memories.

*Funny,* he mused. *I had almost forgotten how painful leaving can be. Over the decades, and in three hospitals along the way, I have left so many parts of myself. When I leave Hilton Head Island, will there be anything left of me?*

Yet, leave he must. His spirit had spoken—again.

Within minutes, Thomas had ascended to the third-floor cardiac unit. No patients, no staff, no distractions. In silence, he walked the empty halls to his office. Embraced by solitude, the doctor could think and reflect.

Once there, Thomas barely glanced at his daily calendar. He knew its contents. No more scheduled surgeries; just hospital rounds, patient follow-ups, and a final, late-afternoon staff meeting.

Moving to the windows Thomas stared into the smoky-black darkness outside. The glass reflected a thin face, dark hair, heavily-wrinkled tan skin, and high cheek bones, with a narrow nose and deeply set brown eyes. Handsome? No. Interesting? Perhaps.

Alone at this early hour, he allowed his mind to travel back thirty-two years in time.

ॐ

Upon graduating from Provo University's Medical Center in Provo, Utah, the young and eager doctor accepted a residency at a Mayo Clinic location in Wisconsin.

That first day he was greeted by a white-haired professor in his middle 60's with matching, white, bushy eyebrows. With a firm handshake, Dr. Carl Jenkins, Dean of Medicine, said, "Thomas, you are the only full-blooded Native American Navajo Indian on our staff. Welcome to the family."

Those first words set the tone for his years working alongside dedicated doctors during grueling 12-to-18-hour shifts. *Mayo taught me to become a surgeon,* Thomas remembered.

With the passing years, a bond of understanding developed between the young Navajo and the long-widowed professor. Over time, Thomas revealed bits and pieces of his early childhood and life with his mother at San Juan pueblo in Northern New Mexico.

"We had dogs, chickens, goats and horses," he laughed. He explained to Professor Jenkins, "On the reservation, young Indian boys are free to hunt and roam the hills and deserts."

When Alice, Thomas's mother, died at the age of twenty-six—from pneumonia—he left the New Mexico pueblo and returned to the hogan of his Navajo grandmother.

In Utah's canyon lands, the long-held traditions of the Navajo people flourished. Young Thomas was allowed to find and explore the high-cliff ruins of his Indian ancestors. He listened and learned why the elders offered signs of reverence to their sacred deities and sang ancient chants to a mythical Spider Woman (believed to have assisted the Navajo people arise from the underworld). He watched the "old ones" perform sacred dances (many of which a white man would never see).

When his dying grandmother summoned him, Thomas entered her adobe hogan through the east-facing doorway, a welcome to the morning sun. He knelt on the hard-packed dirt floor next to her bed as she gave a final blessing.

"My grandson, you will live among the white man and learn his ways. Your destiny is to become a great healer. Find a way to live in harmony within our traditions."

Thomas fulfilled his grandmother's prophecy and became an outstanding doctor. But, after ten successful years at Mayo, he abruptly resigned. In disbelief, his peers and supervisors told him that leaving Mayo was tantamount to committing professional suicide.

"I am not particularly surprised," came the more measured response from Professor Jenkins, who had mentored Thomas since the beginning.

During their last, quiet talk together Thomas said, "Carl, above all people, you know that I am Navajo. The ancient wisdom and traditions of my people are as viable in me as all the years of medical training I have been fortunate to acquire. I am not ungrateful. Your friendship will forever be in my heart."

Carl's bushy eyebrows furled, as they always did when he was thinking. He nodded, musing, *my young friend is trapped between two cultures; the modern world of medicine of which he is now a part, and the long-held beliefs of his Navajo past.*

And so, the professor and the restless young Navajo doctor parted just as they began—as friends.

Carl's next assignment was to UCSF Medical Center in San Francisco. His first years passed quickly. Unexpectedly, a letter from the Mayo Clinic arrived. It related the passing of Professor Emeritus Carl Jenkins. It included an obituary from the local newspaper and outlined the medical accomplishments of his beloved friend.

Thomas took a worn leather folder from his desk. He placed the letter and Carl's obituary on top of a yellowed, decades-old notice of death published in a New Mexico newspaper, the Rio Arriba *Sun Times*—his mother's.

He whispered, "For me, another chapter has closed."

Years passed. Then, once again, Thomas sensed his spiritual and professional paths were in conflict. Dispirited, Thomas was no longer at peace within himself. He craved an escape from the city's noise and lights and its endless miles of concrete buildings.

Again, he resigned. Such behavior confused his colleagues. By their standards, Thomas proffered no acceptable reason for leaving.

They asked, "Why, doctor? Are you ill?" And, "If you need a sabbatical, of course. God knows you have earned it." Thomas was unmoved.

Hilton Head Island's hospital in South Carolina was his next medical location. Quieter than San Francisco, the island's welcome darkness at night calmed his spirit. At this hospital, Thomas' skills advanced. He became recognized as a highly skilled cardiac surgeon.

Years later, Dr. Meadows was still so charmed by the island's beauty, slow pace of living, and warmth of its people, he could not contemplate leaving.

*Might this be a permanent home?* he wondered.

But eventually, restlessness returned. He wondered. *Why leave again, and go where?* Contentment eluded him. He thought *perhaps returning to my ancestral home will bring me peace.*

Thomas left South Carolina after Thanksgiving and arrived in Santa Fe, New Mexico, one day before Christmas. A heavy snowstorm the night before had blanketed the city. Near the historic Plaza of Governors, he found the La Fonda Hotel and checked in.

After dinner, he stepped outside and began walking around the Plaza. It was Christmas Eve. A crowd was forming and Thomas realized they were moving toward the Cathedral of St. Francis of Assisi for the midnight mass. He felt compelled to follow them in.

In the morning, he drove the thirty miles north to the ruins of his mother's home outside the Pueblo of San Juan. Behind the church he found what he was looking for: a century-old graveyard.

In the freezing cold, he shuffled through decaying tumbleweeds, thistle, and debris. Eventually, he found a small slab. He brushed away the snow and dirt on the fallen stone of his mother's grave. Thomas read the simple words:

*Alice M.*

*Navajo woman*

*Is another chapter closing?* he wondered. *What must I still find?*

Throughout the winter, because Thomas wanted to practice medicine, he drove north to Taos Pueblo and assisted at the local Indian hospital or worked in the medical clinic at San Juan Pueblo. During this time, he rented a small, furnished adobe home with exposed beams and a sitting room with a corner (horno) fireplace stacked with cut cedar logs.

After leaving San Juan pueblo one evening, Thomas swung off the highway and abruptly stopped the car. He got out and stared at the distant hills. His mind raced back almost sixty years.

It had been November, just before a frigid dawn, and as a small boy, naked from the waist up, he had huddled with the older Indian men. Stripped to the waist with deer antlers as a headdress, the group chanted while running down the hills toward the Ceremonial Kiva in the center of the pueblo. It was their annual Deer Dance performed to insure a plentiful hunting season.

*I was too young to enter the sacred Kiva,* he smiled; recalling, *Mother welcomed me with hot, red chili stew and Indian fried bread.*

In Santa Fe, the snowy-wet winter continued. Thomas waited until spring. In late April, after packing the Plymouth, he left the charming city, still circled by snow caps on its Sangre de Cristo Mountains.

Thomas drove south skirting the Sandia Mountain range, while avoiding the sprawling desert city of Albuquerque. He understood that his fascination for the magnificent Southwest had not diminished and his compulsion to find his roots remained strong. However, he knew that the many Indian casinos dotting the highway indicated that the culture of his people—was changing.

By June, he had left New Mexico and entered into the canyonlands of Utah. He headed to the Four Corners, the home of the Navajo Nation. Thomas hiked through deserts, slept on arid desert sand, while listening to the calls of night birds and the dog-like yapping of coyote packs after a hunt. Each day he marveled at the deep blue, almost-turquoise sky, which felt so close he could almost touch it.

One morning, turning off from a main highway onto a dirt road, he drove for miles and found himself in a box canyon. In a deep ravine, he heard low bleating and the tinkling of bells. Intrigued, he saw a Navajo woman herding sheep, much as their ancestors had done for centuries.

After hours of driving, Thomas realized he was lost. *Somewhere ahead is my ancestral home,* he thought. *What will I find if I go forward? Should I turn around and accept another assignment in a white man's hospital?*

Thomas struggled with his thoughts. Could he find peace and harmony within the old ways of his people, or had too many years in a white man's world changed him? Did he even know what that meant—the old ways of any of his ancestors?

His inner turmoil continued as he drove on. Along the rim of mountain ridges behind him, thick clouds darkened the sky. Thomas sensed a heavy thunderstorm approaching. He made a decision to go no further. He looked for a place to turn the car around and avoid getting stuck in the soft sand surrounding the road.

At that moment, he noticed a commotion in a dry riverbed about fifty yards away. Below in the arroyo he saw a red, rusty pickup truck.

Nearby, several Indians, four dogs and what appeared to be a small boy were huddled together.

Without thinking, Thomas stopped, grabbed his medical bag, and scrambled down to them. He acknowledged the Indians with a nod. They did the same.

A boy about ten sat on the ground. Thomas asked, "Are you hurt?"

"Yes," the child grimaced. "I fell."

Kneeling down beside him, Thomas ran his hand slowly down the boy's leg. He could not determine if the ankle was broken or just severely sprained. Protectively, the older of the two Indians stepped forward.

Speaking slowly, he said, "I am Carlos. This is my son, José. We are from the Laguna Pueblo."

The Indian looked at the medical bag. "Are you a doctor?"

"Yes," Thomas confirmed. For several moments, Carlos studied him. "Are you Navajo?"

"Yes,"

"From what Clan?"

Thomas said words he had not spoken aloud in decades, "I am Diné from the Bitter Water Clan."

The boy's father nodded and stepped aside. Still kneeling, Thomas said to José, "I have to remove your boot." Although in pain, José did not cry out.

As Thomas cut away the boot, pack-like dogs approached and sniffed him. Thomas understood as a part of Indian life, dogs roam freely. They are protective but not aggressive. By moving away, Carlos had signaled there was no danger. Satisfied, the dogs moved aside, except for a young tan and brown mongrel who continued to sniff at Thomas as he wrapped the boy's ankle in an Ace bandage.

The Doctor wondered, *is this dog thinking I am going to hurt the boy?* He gently pushed the dog away, but it returned quickly and stayed.

"Whose dog is this?" he asked.

"Nobody's," said the boy.

"What's its name?"

"Dog," came the reply.

Later, Thomas said, "José, I do not believe your ankle is broken. But it is badly sprained."

Turning to Carlos, he asked, "Can you take your son to a doctor for an x-ray?"

"No doctor. Only nurse in our pueblo," said Carlos pointing south. "We will go now."

Thomas told José, "Try not to walk on this foot. Let the nurse see it tonight, if you can."

Within minutes, while half-carrying little José, the Indians and dogs were moving toward their pickup.

Getting to his feet, Thomas climbed up from the arroyo. Already the pickup, along with his newest patient, had rumbled up from the arroyo and driven on to the roadway.

Surrounded by vast Southwest desert, Thomas watched the sun's lengthening rays cast shadows while moving along the ridges of distant mountain ranges. He sucked in a deep breath and allowed the clean, warm desert air to fill his nostrils. The heaviness in him seemed to lift. His heart felt light. A sense of balance, which he had so longed to find, seemed to enter his body.

"At last, I am at peace," he murmured.

As he placed the medical bag in the car's back seat, he noticed the brown and tan mongrel sitting inside near the open front window. The irony of the moment did not escape him.

A dog with no name—and a man with no destination.

Thomas eased his long body into the car's front seat. "We've got to give you a name," he chuckled while glancing sideways at the panting dog. Starting the engine, Doctor Thomas Meadows understood there would be no need to turn the car around.

# My Family Tree(s)

### LA Winkle

I learned there are six shallow-rooted trees.
I, too, am a shallow-rooted tree.
My family tree doesn't run deep.
It runs wide and nurses many broken branches.

A *spruce* landed in Nova Scotia in the 1800s.

From there a *maple* flourished
in the Adirondack Mountains
for a few generations.

A *willow* wept in Buffalo
over broken promises and secrets,
its boards warped by racism.

In Appalachia an *ash* crumbled
before a bejeweled, winged force of nature.
Never bent or swayed, just collapsed.
They destroyed the ashes
to protect the forest.

The *cottonwood* called
from the red rocks of Sedona.
Only my brother answered.

Now, a majestic *oak* thrives in the Lowcountry,
draped in Spanish moss, towering,
mighty against gusts and gales,
providing shade and serenity.
Stability for my family.

# Try Harder

Eric Johnson

They said she was once a nun.
Not a Flying Nun from TV
or a singing Nun from the movies
but the ass-kicking kind
from over at Saint Madeline's
where they were paid to beat
the Devil out of you.

I went to public school.
Plenty of devilment, but no nuns
just reckless children
who spread rumors that our English teacher
was so cruel and rigid
she had to be either a nun or a vampire.

I took these lies as truth.
They explained her stiff white blouse
fastened to her neck by a silver stickpin
its shaft the length of a hypodermic.
Her thin lips pressed into a pink line of defense
through which no kindness escaped.
Her eyes, the color of slate
held us in grim suspense
as we stammered through recitations
of *in Just-* by e. e. Cummings and *Lorna Doone.*

Her voice held the comfort
of a feral cat scraping its claws
against a sheet of steel.
She once held an ink splotched page aloft
claiming it contained an entire paragraph
*void of one single period.*
The word *void* frightened me.
Periods filled me with dread.
They always signaled the end.

She hung the keys to Hell on a leather lanyard
that swung from a wooden peg above her desk.
Not Hell exactly but the door to a small office telephone
where she called our mothers
to describe the spelling test where we
misspelled our own names on purpose.
A joint protest against conformity.

I returned to class
after a period of mourning my father's death.
I had forgotten the adolescent axiom:
Be seen, but never get caught being heard.
A boy cut loose
loud and pungent.
I saw his butt leap from his seat
launched by a gaseous lunch
and I laughed like a fool.

Her pink hands flew across the blackboard
listing, in perfect cursive
a forgotten litany of arcane rules
under the title, *Lest We Forget.*

Her head rotated in my direction
an owl tracking its prey
vicious eyes taking my measure
one hand behind her back
the other writing on the board.

I couldn't shake the image.
A farting Jack-in-the-box
welcoming my return to school.
She approached with shark eyes
and thin lips
her wire-rimmed eyeglasses
reflecting terror rays
while her disembodied hands
still up front, guided chalk across the board.
I dug my chin into my chest
acted like I was choking back a cough
thought, *She can't slaughter a sick child.*

I dared to look as she turned
her owl-like head toward the door.
Her voice hissed through dry lips
*Rise sir and diagram the sentence*
*at the board. Give us something*
*we ALL may laugh at.*
I rose with no memory of lines and slashes
or parts of speech.

She left the room.
Through the long pane of glass
I saw the scene unfold.
She stood on her toes

arms extended toward
my mother.
My Mother
in her long black widow coat
and the raven-colored scarf
that brought out the worry in her face.
She held my mother in her chalk-coated grasp
and whispered something too faint for me to hear.
They stood there holding one another.
Eyes closed, foreheads touching, tears mingling.
My teacher mouthed words I took to be sacred.

She returned to class
straightened her grey suit coat,
adjusted the deadly stickpin
cleared her throat the way teachers
do when they don't want you to know
the depths of your ignorance
and their inability to correct it.

She examined my effort.
Glanced at me without expression.
Corrected my work with contempt and said,
"Your mother will need you to try harder now."

# EVOLUTION

*Sea Turtle* | Lindsay Pettinicchi

# Shoes Don't Make the Player

Eric Johnson

The old cedar chest in our basement held the trappings that signified the beginning and end of each season. Lifting its heavy lid allowed your hopes to rise along with the musty smell of picnic blankets, summer sandals, and a fraying straw beach bag. My father unearthed his war-torn pair of Jack Purcell sneakers from beneath a moth-eaten quilt. He revealed them with a ritualistic flourish, banging them against each other to shake out last summer's sand. He flexed them to release the tension in the dry rotting canvas and stuffed his hands inside to dislodge hidden pebbles. He gazed at them with reverence, perhaps wondering what other shoes could handle the rigor of washing a '57 Chevy and minutes later take a turn at bat during a stickball game.

I wondered why he never replaced his sneakers each season. I held the hope that he'd buy a new pair and spring for a stylish pair for me. This was ludicrous because my father was a man of whom it was said, "Popeye can work a dollar harder than any man I know." He held onto those old sneakers like they were precious gems. He owned work boots that he wore as a smelter at the United States Mint, and a pair of dress shoes for church, but I can't remember him owning a different pair of sneakers. Today he'd be called a minimalist with his own podcast where he extolled the virtues of owning practically nothing. Back then he was just Pop.

I'm not sure how he acquired the Jack Purcells, a name brand shoe designed by a Canadian badminton champion. I imagined wealthy industrialists wearing them while sipping cocktails at the cricket club. The Purcells didn't seem like casual footwear favored by a smelter who drank Schmidt's beer while playing checkers on his front porch. Their existence, however, put the thought in my mind that my old man might understand my need to wear a culturally popular pair of sneakers.

While Pop sat on the trunk attempting to slide what remained of his feet into his Jack Purcells, I asked him why he never bought a new pair. He leaned back against the cement wall and took a long drag from his Winston. "Well, Rick," he began. "If you weren't playing at the Christian Street Y, you weren't playing nowhere. Now... I played for Central High back when it was Central Manual. But the real games were down at Christian Street. I played against Stretch Rex, Eggy Brock, Charles "Tarzan" Cooper, and Zach Clayton. Man, those boys could play. Tarz Cooper played for the Harlem Rens. That's right. The mighty New York Renaissance."

"Wow," I replied, rubbing my eyes, straining to pay attention, wondering what this had to do with his reluctance to buy new sneaks.

"Yes, sir. I played for the Philadelphia Panthers the year we shut out the Hell Fighters. We beat the Athenians too. I guarded Stretch Rex. I used to step on Stretch's big feet so that he couldn't jump."

There was no stopping Pop once he was on a roll.

"You know, Rick, my dad—your Grandpop—only came to one of my games. He worked at Campbells Soup out in Camden and could never get off. But he made it to one game at Christian Street. The guy I was playing against, who was it? I think it was Buss King. That guy was giving it to me pretty good. I had scratches and bruises all over. He hit me in the gut, doubled me over. I went back at him. We both got put out the game. You know what your Grandpop said?"

I knew because this story came up whenever anyone living in the house got into a fight. Before I could answer, Pop rose to his feet and announced, "He said, 'Son, you done alright till you hit that boy.'"

I laughed appropriately as Pop squeezed the top of my head, chuckled, and climbed the stairs.

Looking at Pop's decrepit Jack Purcells was a reminder that my own sneaks were badly in need of replacement. My boyhood self-esteem was tied to the brand of gym shoe known as Chuck Taylor All Stars. Check out any black-and-white photograph of Wilt Chamberlain and you'll see The Big Dipper wearing white high-top Chucks. Only corny little kids wore other nameless brands purchased by thrifty mothers at the local grocery store. If you went outside in new sneakers that were considered lame, someone would holler "Stompsies!" and every boy in hearing distance would stomp your new shoes and your feet into oblivion. I had advanced from being a babyish 10-year-old and was desperate for a legit pair of sneakers. I poked my finger through the sole of my right shoe and showed it to my mother. She accused me of purposely vandalizing the shoe and told me to show my father, who was sitting in the living room enjoying a cigarette and the evening paper.

"Pop. Look at this." I wiggled my index finger through the hole in the sole.

Pop put the newspaper on his lap and asked to see the shoe. I handed it to him, and he put his long finger inside and asked, "So, where's the cardboard?"

"What?" I asked.

He showed me his sneakers which had dissolved into an unnatural shade of grey. The shoelaces were segments of broken strands, cobbled together to form a semblance of their original length. The rubber soles were nearly transparent. He took off one shoe and said, "They ain't broke-in good until you got some cardboard in there." He saw my dejection and laughed. "I'm just kidding. We'll get you a pair of shoes next time we hit Sears. How's that?"

That wasn't good. Sears sold a brand of sneaker suspiciously named "The Jeeper." They looked like Chuck Taylors, but they had a label in the back and an emblem on the ankle which clearly read "Sears Jeepers," I had seen kids humiliated for wearing Jeepers, so I lied, maybe even forced out a tear. "Mom says I gotta get new sneakers. Chuck Taylors, 'cause they last longer."

My older brothers, who were lounging in the living room fighting over the comics and sports page, heard my fib and scattered like canines at a fox hunt. They knew what was coming and couldn't bear the 1,000th retelling of how the Philly Panthers rode a million miles eating sardines out of a can to somewhere in the mountains to play the "Good for Nothins" in Bohunk, New York.

A look of skepticism shrouded Pop's face. "Chuck Taylors, eh?" He used his size 13 foot to push the hassock toward me. "Sit down, Rick."

I stared at the small stool like it was the judgment seat.

"Sit," he coughed. I sat down and stared up at him as he glared at me through the haze of a freshly lit Winston.

"Son, back in my barnstorming days, we used to have to ride for hours in an unheated jalopy through the White Mountains of New Hampshire. We put on everything we had to stay warm. Wore our sweats over our street clothes and bundled up in our overcoats, but there was nothing you could do for your feet. It got so bad one night I think a couple of my toes were ready to drop off. But, when we got to the old barn where we were supposed to play, that's just what we did, we played. It was either that or starve. I got out there and ran on frozen feet. My dogs ain't been right since. That's why I don't spend a whole lot of money on fancy shoes."

He told me to lean in close, which I did. He slipped out of his sneakers and tore off his socks to reveal his grey, peeling tootsies.

I tumbled backwards off of the hassock, afraid I'd be overcome by the deadly stench I imagined came from his withered toes.

I could hear my older brothers laughing from the stairway as Pop tossed his socks at me and said, "Look, a hunk of skin just fell off!"

After I recovered from my shock, he said, "The shoes don't make the player, son; the player makes the shoes. If you can play in Chuck Taylors, you can play in Jeepers."

While I was undergoing my fashion trauma, Pop began coaching an industrial league team for the US Mint that my mother called "The Plug Nickels." I served as his assistant, working the scorer's table and handing out water and towels to the men he coached. They were all US Mint workers who talked endlessly of serving in Korea (which they pronounced KOE-rear and someplace they called "the European lands." They wore tattoos depicting battleships, playing cards, dice, and one man had a semi-erotic drawing of a woman named Dot on his right bicep. He could make her dance when he flexed his muscles. They would give me a quarter for keeping an eye on their equipment bags, one of which held a pint of gin for halftime and the cigarettes they'd smoke during time-outs. My dad's coaching strategy was simple, "Fellas! You gotta put the ball in the hole!"

It struck me as strange that the fellas listened to his stories. When he removed his socks to make his frostbite summation, they stared at his feet with awe and nodded with compassion. The team celebrated after every game—win or lose—at a place called The 800 Club. I'd sit near the front door with the ball between my legs, nursing a glass of Coke, staring at my dilapidated sneakers. It was during one of these "team meetings" that a fellow snatched the ball from me and began dribbling furiously. He spun the ball on one finger in my face. When I tried to grab it, he rolled the ball up his arm, across his back shoulder, and down the other arm. Then he placed it back in my lap.

"What's wrong, little man," he huffed. I looked down at my feet and he looked down too. Then he yelled, "Hey Popeye, when you gonna break down and buy this boy some real kicks!" Everyone laughed, including Pop, who tried to save face by mumbling something about shoes not making the player, blah blah and so on. Everyone booed. "Come on now, Popeye. You know that ain't right. You gonna mess around and get your boy's feet stomped off."

My dad was a union shop steward, so he knew when to bend to

the will of the workers. Either that or he was embarrassed for being thought of as a tightwad. It didn't matter because he took me to the Army Navy Store where he plunked down $6.50 for a pair of white low-top Chuck Taylor All Stars. I nursed those shoes well past their expiration date, knowing that they, like my dad's old Jack Purcells, would be very hard to replace.

*Converse now owns the manufacturing rights to Chuck Taylor All Stars and Jack Purcells.*

# Finding My Swing

### Phil Lindsey

It seems as if I've lost my swing.
I can't find it anywhere.
I'm frustrated, aggravated,
pulling out my hair!

I've spent a fortune on instruction,
taken lessons every week.
Did you see that brand new Calloway?
It's on order as we speak.

I've read all the books, watched videos,
bought every training-aid devised,
played and practiced every day—
I've even *exercised!*

St. Andrew must be busy.
He must not have heard my prayer.
I can't believe our Patron Saint
really doesn't care.

All these things, to no avail;
my swing eludes me still.
*You're swaying,* someone told me.
Oh, man, if looks could kill.

But last week on the driving range
came the deepest cut of all.
The Head Pro watched me swing and said,
*You should take up pickleball.*

*Golf Swing* | Phil Lindsey

# Montauk 1977

Susan Hearty

This weekend, I learned that Brian Mulligan had died. I had to keep re-reading the notice. Somehow, it stunned me. Other people I knew had died before. A few years earlier, I had seen that my best friend from junior high had passed away. I mourned who we had been and our never-to-be repaired distance. Death was no longer the surprise it had been. But Brian's death pushed me back into a time I thought I had moved past. It was that summer immediately after college, when I felt freedom, fear, and expectation. I had no job and no real idea of where I was heading. I had to do something. On the other hand, it was summer and I needed what might be my last vacation time for decades.

I hadn't really known Brian in high school. We mixed in different circles. He was a year older and a football player. He wasn't quite fat but rather pudgy, the type of guy I call vanilla pudding, bland features swallowed in his face, outstanding only in his vanilla-ness. Our paths crossed afterwards, at a party in Montauk of all places, far from our hometown in so many ways.

High school had been hard for me. It's all about fitting in and I did not. I read a lot and had very specific ideas about life and fashion. I grew up in Levittown and, while its reputation for cookie-cutter houses may have been undeserved, at that time its population was very homogeneous. Homes were filled with large Catholic families, the children clones, little rubber stamps, one after another. I remember going to a party a few years back and a guy asked me if I knew who he was. He laughed when I said, "A Connelly?" Indeed. Which Connelly, I was unsure of. He was the Connelly from my brother's year, not the one from mine.

I was a nerd, though the word wasn't used at the time nor was it in any way trendy or acceptable. I was left-leaning in a community that for the most part revered Richard Nixon. I used to stand on the main thoroughfare with a peace sign in front of the armed forces recruiting station. Many years later, I attended a reunion dinner where Richard Nixon's resignation was mourned. This was the land where I lived. I had left as soon as I could for an out-of-state university.

I returned home briefly after college graduation and ran into Mikey O'Connor at the local watering hole. A year older than me and definitely not in my set, Mikey was a former football player whose high school yearbook photo depicted him like one of those rabid English soccer fans with hobnail boots—so not my type. When he approached me at the bar on that early summer evening, though, he'd changed a bit and looked less the yob. My friend Laura hissed at me, "That's Mikey O'Connor!" She adored football players. Even so, I was the one Mikey asked out.

The fourth of July 1977 was on the horizon and there was going to be a group from high school going to Montauk for the weekend. Montauk at that time was still definitely the un-Hamptons. We were Levittown, still gritty and blue-collar, lower middle-class. Brian Mulligan had become a charter boat captain and had a house there which was to be the base for the weekend.

I told Mikey I had to ask my dad if I could go, but when I asked my father was furious with me—not because I wanted to go with Mikey to Montauk, but rather because I had said I needed his permission. I had just returned from being away for four years. My father asked if I had been away would I have gone. Yes, definitely. So, why ask? This set the foundation so that, in the following years, I came and went as I pleased. I was an anomaly in that era and that space.

Mikey and I drove out early in the morning. It was a two-and-a-half-hour drive without traffic, with the landscape and the light changing significantly as we headed east. People were already there when we arrived at Brian's little house on some side street with a fairly large unkempt yard. The crowd was one from high school that had never been my friends—football players and cheerleaders. Since I had left high school and Levittown, I had blossomed. Well, everyone does, don't they? You leave behind high school, teenage hormones, and expectations. I had shed my glasses and emerged from my chrysalis. They saw me as a new thing, not the high school me.

We walked in and were immediately handed beers. I grew up in the era where everyone in Levittown drank. It was a fact of life. You went over to someone's parent's house and you were immediately given alcohol. At that age, I was very good at holding onto a drink and/or pouring it out. I was still fascinated and slightly intimidated by the former cheerleaders chugging beers in their short shorts, gushing and smiling. I remember Crosby, Stills, and Nash on what appeared to be a continuous loop on the stereo. In those days, there were record players and probably everyone was too drunk to change the record.

Like me, our host Brian had also undergone a metamorphosis in recent years. Now Brian was lean and tan, with beach-bleached blond hair and deep green eyes. He was gorgeous and charming, and I was stunned and tongue tied. His girlfriend was one of the former cheerleaders and unexpectedly very friendly to me. By evening, with the guests bleary and passing out, and the air thick with the smell of cigarette smoke and beer, Brian approached Mikey and suggested that we leave and go across town to his boat. It was the era where we still drank and drove. Driving while drunk was our norm and not enough of us had yet died for it to register.

Remember the excitement and newness of being "adult" couples? It was so grown up to leave the others behind. The boat was moored and the dock relatively silent after the party noise back at the house. We drank more and then Mikey and I retired to a berth fueled by hormones, alcohol, and excitement. My outstanding memory of the evening was looking through the porthole and seeing the 4th of July fireworks exploding over the water. Mikey thought I was seeing fireworks because of him.

Eventually we all passed out, rising the next morning to more beer and sunshine, then drifting off home. Mikey and I continued dating for the summer, although I didn't like him or dislike him. I went along with the flow, as it enhanced my reputation in certain circles to be known as the girl Mikey was seeing. What little romance there was faded along with the summer.

Ready for a more glamorous and arduous lifestyle, a few months later I started down my path by beginning work in New York City. I put Levittown or, as some of us called it "Leave-it-town,", behind me. Or did I? The reverberations from that Montauk 4th of July lived on. An old high school friend came for a visit years later and his first question was about that party. He had heard about it from one of the Mulligan brothers all the way out in California. Over the years that holiday weekend had assumed mythic proportions. Apparently, it was the last time the high school crowd came together before moving on with the rest of their lives. It became a memory of a rosy time.

We all still know each other. It was that kind of place. You never get away no matter how much distance, physical and otherwise, you think you may have gone. We hold onto those associations because these are the people who know who we were. It's these ties that reach through time. But after that Montauk weekend I never saw Brian Mulligan again, just remembered his deep green eyes and the kindness he had shown to me. Now he—like that time—was gone forever. I loved that summer when life was still full of possibilities. The air was warm and the nights started late and stretched to soft dawns, scented with liquor. It was the summer when lines blurred. Football and art could intersect. Life started to move beyond high school, and "adult" became an identity. There were fireworks to be seen in Montauk.

# Triboluminescence

Kyle Zubatsky

Lightening rocks rest on my mantle,
discovered in sandy arroyos.
Primordial relics carry secrets.

In a lightless closet, door shut tight,
stones strike with violent friction.
Over and over the quartz grinds.

Air thickens with ominous sulfur.
Yellow sparks fracture the air--
embers with no heat.

Cold magic fills the blackness.
Silicon gems glow from inside--
a glimpse of torment.

Or is it my imagination ...

Faces press against crystal.
Lips release anguished cries.
No sound escapes mineral walls.
The clash ceases. Rocks grow dim.

Contorted flesh disappears.
Opened mouths close in defeat.
Rocks return to the shelf.
Centuries of secrets fade.

They wait.

# The Spinach Wars

Hiyaguha Cohen

My mother lied to me. I distinctly remember her hovering over me at the dinner table when I was a kid, dumping green slop from a can onto my plate. "Eat your spinach," she would say. "It'll make you strong like Popeye." I managed to choke the slime down, year after year, because I believed in Popeye. I wanted to transform from a knobby weakling into a hulk after a shot of spinach, so I would no longer be the shortest, skinniest kid in my class.

Now that I'm well-entrenched in advanced age, I'm still a shrimp—and shrinking. Why? Because the spinach thing was a hoax. Turns out canned spinach has virtually no nutritional value; plus, dangerous metals leach from the can into the green goo and cause 7,032 types of cancer and brain disease. Fresh spinach isn't much better. It's a calcium-blocking weed, full of nasty oxalic acid.

Of course, spinach wasn't the only revolting food Mom served in the name of nutrition. How many cups of chalky milk did she force me to drink? How many slabs of liver did I ingest? How many soft-boiled eggs did I gag on? All in vain. All because Mom said I could have dessert if I finished eating the crap on my plate. Now it turns out the stuff she made me eat is all bad, bad, bad. Milk is laden with harmful hormones, liver is a fatty no-no, and eggs are a cholesterol nightmare. I would have been better off going straight for the ice cream and skipping the preliminaries ... as I always dreamed of doing.

The taste of canned spinach has long since faded from my palate, and after years of psychotherapy, I've been able to forgive Mom for making me eat it. She couldn't help her ignorance. What I can't forgive is the lie she told me about desserts: When I grew up and no longer lived under her roof, I could eat as much junk as I wanted.

Naturally, I couldn't wait to grow up. I figured adulthood would be an orgy of Good Humor pops, Hershey's bars, and ice-cream sodas day and night. And so, I rushed through childhood breathlessly, visions of Sugar Babies dancing in my head. Funny I never noticed how the adults I knew avoided desserts completely.

The cruel truth, of course, is the adult body can't assimilate junk foods. Now that I'm finally able to afford all the desserts I can fit in the basket—with no Mom around to shake her finger at me—I have to watch my weight, cellulite, cholesterol, blood sugar, and trace mineral levels.

I finally know the real reason grown-ups don't allow kids to indulge in wanton candy revelry: They're jealous. Kids can drink two milkshakes every day for a year and still look like twigs with mouths. If I drank two milkshakes every day for a year, I'd end up with eighty-nine-inch hips and the Self-Made Diabetic of the Year award.

To make matters worse, now that I've reached the age when there's all this pressure to be GC (gastronomically correct), treats keep getting better and better. Ring Dings have given way to tiramisu, store-brand ice cream has been upstaged by Ben and Jerry's, and Fig Newtons have evolved into Tates and Mint Milanos. We now have croissants and scones, tortes and tarts, chocolate ganache and biscotti. Whoever heard of such things when I was a kid? Then, graham crackers were good enough, and gummy bears were God.

It isn't fair. I ate canned vegetables and settled for Wheaties instead of Frosted Flakes, and now I want my reward. I was promised I could eat all the sweets I wanted when I grew up, and damn it, I'm going to get my fill. I just won't advertise my vice. I'll keep a perfectly straight face and say, "I watch my diet and exercise every day, but I just can't lose those inches."

The game hasn't changed since childhood. Then I'd tiptoe into the kitchen after Mom went to sleep and grab a mouthful of Mallomars. If there were no cookies in the house, I'd settle for Ex-Lax in desperation. At least it was chocolate. Now I say, "Just a little sliver, please" and then slink back to enjoy another sliver and another and another until the whole cake is gone. Or I tell myself, "These are low-fat cookies, so I can have forty-seven of them, topped with low-fat ice cream and fat-free whipped cream, and maybe a dollop of real hot fudge."

I can't help it: I need sweets. How else can I deal with the horrible truth that adulthood is not at all as much fun as Popeye made it out to be? Anyway, I bet Popeye didn't really eat spinach. I bet he filled those spinach cans with green licorice and just pretended because some grown-up paid him to do so.

# Snowy Egrets Roost

Gloria Krolak

Snowy egrets roost;

starched handkerchiefs drying

on clotheslines at dusk.

# A Cab Goes to Harlem

Richard Kammen

It was September 1969—a crisp, cloudless New York Sunday. I enjoyed driving the cab on Sundays. Good traffic flow. Possible airport runs and good money. Not much hassle on Sunday mornings. Sundays and the two evenings a week I drove the cab provided a welcome respite from the competitive boredom of law school.

I was driving uptown, trolling for fares among the White and wealthy. In the mid-80s on the East side, I saw a mocha-skinned woman dressed in a straight blue skirt and white blouse. In my memory, she was wearing a blue Jackie Kennedy pillbox hat.

I am ashamed to admit that while driving the cab, I did racial profiling before it became known as a staple of police work. At the time, I would have said it was about not wanting to go to certain areas where I could not get a fare back. Or just being careful because many cabs were robbed in those days. That was the lie I was telling myself. But the truth is I often drove by African Americans looking for White passengers out of prejudice.

I don't know what was different that day, but when I saw the mocha woman in the blue skirt, white blouse, and pillbox hat, I slowed, checked her out, and stopped. She did not immediately grab the rear door handle of the Checker cab. She came to the front window and looked me over.

Before I could bolt from this breach of driver/passenger etiquette, she was in the backseat.

"Sir, would you like to make some money off the meter?"

The only possible answer to her question was "Yes. Money off the meter was the best money as the cab company would not get its share."

She took a breath. "Here is the situation. I live in Harlem.

And, of course, there are no cabs there. Most of the people in our building go to the same church, but for some, walking is difficult, so if you'll drive us, we'll pay you ten dollars per trip. There will be four, maybe five trips."

Sunday morning. Middle-aged or elderly passengers. Off the meter.

"Sure, why not. You pay the fare from here to the building?"

It was a shamefully abusive demand, but she did not hesitate. "Of course."

So we drove to 137th Street, and she filled the cab while I drove to a church that was maybe ten blocks away. In my memory, it was an AME church. I dropped folks off and went back to get another load. When we were done, the mocha lady, who by now I knew to be "Sister Alice," said, "Church will be over in a couple of hours. We'll do the same coming home. That okay?"

I made close to a hundred dollars—big, big money in those days. We agreed I would be at the building the following Sunday and on Sundays from then on. For most of the next year, my Sundays were a cash cow.

One of the benefits of driving a cab is the driver is often invisible to the passenger. People would have amazing, sometimes shocking conversations in front of the stranger driving them from here to there. Sexual escapades, complaints about work, home, school, the boss, the husband, the wife. No topic was off-limits because the driver was both invisible and deaf.

Sister Alice's friends were no different. There was gossip about who was sleeping with whom. "And I don't think there was too much sleeping going on." And whose son was in jail or whose daughter was "in trouble." But they also spoke of the slights, the routine insults. In 1969, what we call the N-word was common even in polite society. For these poor souls, that offensive word was heard every day. And in time, I understood how much that word hurt. If they said someone was "pure Alabama," invariably, they were speaking of a White person, and "pure Alabama" was no compliment. I was ashamed. They could have been talking about me.

After a few months, Sister Alice said, "Brother Richard, would you join us for services?"

I am a proudly backsliding, revolving-door Jew. In on Rosh Hashanah, out on Yom Kipper. Some years, I only made half the circle. Some years, I did not enter the door at all. I'd only been to Christian services a few times. Those were at White churches. I had no idea what I was in for.

When I went into the church, my presence caused a hear-a-pin-drop silence, until someone whispered, "It's okay. It's the cab driver." After that, the room was loud with chatter and laughter. But when the choir began singing, the congregation began clapping, the minister began shouting, and people stood and praised Jesus. It was beyond my imagination. I am sure I was sitting in slack-jawed amazement at the fervor, the beauty, the noise, and the joy.

That spring, Brother Charles died.

"Of course, you'll join us and pay your respects."

When I die, I want to have a funeral like the one held for Brother Charles. I want people falling in grief; I want tears cascading until they are dripping off chins. I would like some of the bereaved, overcome by pain, to try to get into the coffin with me. And I want those who come to my funeral to have the food that was served in the basement of the church. I hope they'll enjoy the macaroni, the greens, the salads, the ham, the chicken, and the brown bags holding half-pints of whiskey.

When I go, that is what I want. Loud singing, roll-on-the-floor grief, good food, and hooch. A perfect sendoff.

As the following summer approached, I left New York to get married and clerk for an Indianapolis law firm. To my shame, after returning to New York for my final year of law school, I did not visit my friends. At the time, I considered my experience driving

Sister Alice and her friends an interesting adventure into a world I'd never seen. A world, that in my privilege, I did not appreciate.

Only later did I understand the gifts those kind, devout, brave people gave me. Only as my life and career brought me into increased contact with African Americans did I see that Harlem in 1969 was no different from Indianapolis where I'd grown up and to which I returned after graduation. Only then did I begin to understand that the slights and abuse Sister Alice, Brother Charles, and their clan endured were the same indignities my black colleagues and clients encountered. And I am ashamed, head-bowed ashamed, to acknowledge that before I met Sister Alice and her friends, I inflicted some of those indignities.

I have said many times I learned more about how to be a lawyer while driving that cab than I ever learned in law school. And I think now that wheeling that cab in Harlem, I began to dimly understand the impact prejudice had on Sister Alice, Brother Charles, and my other friends.

I see now that there was, and perhaps still is, a seed of prejudice in me I must constantly work to root out. I am embarrassed that for much of my youth that seed flourished. I believe the vine of prejudice began to be starved in that cab, in that church, with those lovely, wonderful giving people.

And I am grateful to fate, karma, serendipity, God—or whatever caused me to stop to pick up the mocha-skinned lady wearing the blue skirt, white blouse, and blue pillbox hat.

# Odyssey

Jessica Goody

Hatchlings emerge from fragile
eggshells, cracked shards like broken china
embedded in the sand. The beach is strewn
with kelp that glows like radium, a lighted
path to the sea. Twitching forward
like clockwork toys, they move blindly
towards its rhythmic breath,
fresh and bitter with seaweed and salt.
They struggle from shell to water,
strain towards life, towards freedom.
Narrow tracks dot the damp shore, an exodus
of tiny Bedouins crossing the desert.

# VARIATIONS

*Watchful* | Cathy Bateman

# A Free Heart

Hiyaguha Cohen

We were three at the beach. My partner, Trek, his 43-year-old sister, Jojo, and me. I mention Jojo's age because it happened to be her birthday on June 25, and she wanted to catch the sunrise. She said her energies were activated because birthdays invigorate people, make their energies come alive. She also said she knew the Goddess was pleased with her. Otherwise, why would it be 78 degrees outside, her favorite temperature?

We stood on the shoreline letting the warm water lap our feet, staring at the still-dark horizon. When the glowing dot of light broke through the slate sky, Jojo cried.

"I can't bear the beauty," she said. Then she danced, swirling multicolored scarves around her body, lifting her long skirt, extending her arms to the breeze. I turned my camera from her to the sea.

She danced into my field of vision. I tried not to be annoyed—it was her birthday, after all. *I should take her picture,* I told myself. *It would make a pretty photo with her long hair blowing in the breeze and the swirly scarves and all.* Instead, I announced I was taking a walk and headed along the shore at a brisk pace.

Ten minutes toward Folly Beach, I needed a bathroom. I took the path to the Omni Hilton Head and entered the air-conditioned wonderland. Hotel bathrooms often delighted me with their marble excesses and guest towels. *What kind of person are you who likes bathrooms but rejects your own sister-in-law?*

I caught a glimpse in the mirror. Hair askew from the wind, facial crags pronounced in the fluorescent clarity. If the permanent frown lines etched like landmarks around my chin could speak, they'd say, "Bitch."

The breeze blew with more enthusiasm on the return walk. I

kept my head down to prevent hair from whipping my face, kicking through the shallow water as I ambled along the shore. Then I came to a curly-haired girl, maybe six years old, holding a scallop shell.

"Look!" she said to me, extending her hand to share her gift.

"That's beautiful," I said.

I intended to keep walking, but she stepped in front of me.

"I have a dog," she said.

"That's nice."

"His name is Barney. He ate my crayons."

"Did he get sick?"

"We had to take him to the *bet*."

"Poor Barney."

I attempted to resume my journey, but the child was a barnacle. I glanced around for a parent. Up the beach, a couple sat on a blue blanket, watching, smiling. I could swear I heard them say, "Isn't she killer cute?" I knew they didn't mean me.

"You wanna see me dance?" the girl asked.

*Not really*, I thought, but she yelled, "Wait!" as she ran on kid-skinny legs up to the blanket and grabbed her mother's wrap. She spun down the sand with the wrap flapping, a swirling dervish, finishing with a pirouette at my feet.

*A Jojo in training*, I thought as the girl implored me to join her.

"Dance with me!" she said, laughing.

"I have to get back to my partner. He's waiting for me."

She ignored my objection and grabbed my hand, pulling me along, and when I didn't move as she hoped, she took the wrap off and draped it over my head like a kaftan.

"You look so pretty!" she said. "Dance."

I flapped my arms a few times and started to remove the wrap when she did a full-on arabesque and told me to follow her. *Oh, what the heck.* I swirled the chiffon, and when she laughed, I twirled and took a leap. Out about a hundred yards, a dolphin surfaced. The girl pointed and took my hand. And then, Jojo and Trek walked toward us.

"Hey, we were getting worried," Trek said. But Jojo didn't seem the least concerned as she ran toward us to join in the dance. The girl let go of me and took Jojo's hands. They danced together, leaping, swirling, laughing.

I told my mind to shut up. It was saying, *You don't just go up to random kids and cavort with them* and *It's one thing for a kid to dance on the beach, but a grown woman?*

And then Jojo and the girl fell into the sand laughing, and the girl sat up.

"I have cancer," the girl said. "You want to be my friend?"

Jojo held her hands up, palms facing outward, and signaled the girl to put her palms against hers.

"What's your name?" Jojo asked.

"Melanie."

"Melanie, I vow to be your forever and loyal friend. If you ever get scared or lonely, think about dancing on the beach with me."

Then she pulled Melanie in for a full body hug and said, "You want to dance some more?"

When I got home, I printed the photo I took of the dancers and framed it. Now, whenever I get scared or lonely or notice a new worry line on my brow, I pull out the photo. I think about Jojo dancing on the beach and wonder how even a dolphin knew a free heart was nearby.

# Leave Me Alone!

Denise K. Spencer

Keys in hand, I run out the door.
The visitor arrives.
*I don't have time for this!*
*Leave me alone!*
   *Okay, okay. I'll give you five minutes.*

A deadline looms. Focus is my friend.
The visitor returns.
*I can't manage this now!*
*Leave me alone!*
   *Okay, okay. I'll jot down that concept.*

A critical board discussion is underway.
The visitor returns.
*This is a terrible time!*
*Leave me alone!*
   *Okay, okay. I'll make a quick note.*

At last, I start to sink into sleep,
but the visitor returns.
There is no point in protest.
I rise, make coffee,
and become the grateful hostess.
With submission and joy,
I welcome the poem
   that won't
     leave me alone.

**Grace | Jo Paduch**

# Ancient Trees

Jessica Goody

The trees have grown old together,
a coven of seers and sages. Gray
moss drips from the bones of their
brittle branches. Knobbed and spotted
with age, they toss their tangled
hag's hair with reckless dash against
the breeze. Ancient trees whisper
secrets with every hiss of wind.
We cannot hear their verdant voices,
only feel their truths straining to be told.
They remain, endure, abide, ageless
observers of humanity's endless cruelty.
Generations of soldiers poised on a hill,
brass buttons shining and muskets firing,
leaving silent witnesses scarred by shrapnel.
The trees saw the elegant ships, sails
taut and gleaming like silk shirt-fronts,
bearing the cringing cargo of slaves.
Storm-torn and stripped by wind,
ancient trees bear their bark with pride,
their broken limbs now ragged and arthritic,
ravaged by the scar-deep fissures of time.

# Pluff Mud

Susan Diamond Riley

that familiar smell hits
at the Lowcountry bridges
arched high over falling tide

inhale deeply
embrace the earthy tang
marsh grass and salty sea

fusion of life and death
decaying creatures and spent spartina
nourish oyster beds above

Carolina dolphins slide ashore
lunchtime feast
on slick banks

heavenly pluff mud
sharp scent of the Sea Islands
sweet aroma of home

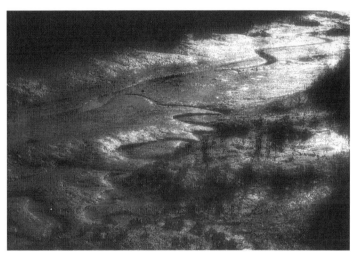

*Pluff Mud* | Rick VanDette

# Pluff Dog

Suzie Eisinger

Week after week, we drove to the Humane Society, searching for the newest canine arrivals and lingering by the cages of the many dogs that remained. My kids, now teenagers, had never had a dog before, so choosing the right one was big. Besides field trips to PetSmart to check out all the necessary (and not so necessary) gear for a dog, they spent hours researching the qualities and breeds that would make the best pet for our family. Checklists were made, but no dogs could be found that matched their hefty set of criteria: older, calm, not too big, well-behaved, non-shedding (okay, that was mine), good with people and other dogs. Bonus—likes to chase balls on the beach.

We kept returning, hoping there was one dog we had somehow overlooked. One meant only for us among the long lineup of eager, hopeful pets awaiting their chance at the shelter.

And then, on our fourth visit, we met Jasper. He was a whirling dervish of energy, whimpering and scampering around us as we knelt on the floor of the office to meet him. Medium-sized with a tawny coat and broad chest, he had exotic almond-shaped eyes and a forehead that crinkled when he looked perplexed.

"He's a sweetheart," said the shelter worker, explaining that Jasper had just arrived and was still in quarantine while he was being checked out. In our excitement, it didn't occur to us to ask how he got along with other dogs or any other questions on our checklist. No, that force of nature wound up distracting us from everything but the logistics required to bring him home.

In the weeks that followed, we realized our diligent attempts to construct the ideal-dog checklist had been a dismal failure. Older dog? Calm? Not even close—this one was two years old and brimming with inexhaustible energy. Well-behaved? That one well-meaning neighbor gifted us with a choke collar ("It will make him mind you better, dear") and another had offered the name of a great trainer ("She worked miracles with my dogs") were our first indications that perhaps it was the inmate running the asylum and not the other way around. We also discovered Jasper was adept at opening doors—balancing his paws on the lever knobs throughout the house and leaning in or out, depending on the direction that would grant him escape. Did I mention that teenagers aren't always good at remembering to lock doors? Jasper capitalized on their mistakes every time.

Still, I could have lived with these *qualities*. The trait that almost finished me off was Jasper's propensity to run away. It didn't matter *why*—the simple act of chasing a squirrel or a green anole was reason enough. Or *where*, for that matter—just as long as it was away from us at high speed, resembling a game of tag—a game we clearly had no hope of winning. Jasper would occasionally stop for a few moments as we gained ground on him, and then, with a look of delight, pivot at the last second and take off in an entirely new direction. This game could go on for half an hour.

One night, as I stretched my legs out on the couch after a particularly long day, my daughter ran in, an alarmed look on her face.

"Jasper got loose."

"*Of course, he did.*" I groaned as I pulled myself up and listened to her explanation of how. After she removed his leash from a walk and pressed the button to close the garage door, he made a fast break and slipped under the door within inches of it closing.

*I am going to kill this dog*, I promised myself resolutely, thinking dark, very un-Mom-worthy thoughts as I walked down the street shouting his name along with my daughter and son, who had fanned out in different directions. After ten minutes, my anger morphed into concern and then fear. What if he had been hit by a car? Or had fallen into the marshy creek, which bordered our neighborhood? *No, he hates the water,* I reminded myself. *He would stay away from the marsh at all costs.*

My daughter caught up with me, her worried face proof enough that Jasper still hadn't been spotted. Together, we walked down the road, occasionally shouting his name, but more often just listening for signs of him—the jangle of his collar, his bark, *anything*.

And then we heard a yelp. Faint and faraway. We stood stock-still waiting for the sound to repeat so we could discern its source. Finally, it did—coming from behind a house three doors down from ours. As we tore through the front and backyard with little concern for trespassing, we heard another yelp and found Jasper neck-deep in pluff mud just beyond our neighbor's dock.

My daughter took a running leap and landed in the mud next to the immobilized dog, managing to get herself stuck in the process. For those who have not experienced the visceral qualities of pluff mud, it is like quicksand—only darker and much smellier. We had no idea how our water-phobic dog managed to end up in the marsh—perhaps he was chasing a squirrel and went off course. However, judging by how deeply he was submerged, we assumed his struggles to escape had only made matters worse.

I stepped gingerly into the mud while holding firmly to the dock for leverage. Reaching out, I caught my daughter's hand and, as she held onto Jasper's collar, dragged them both slowly through the sludge. One by one, they clambered out, accompanied by the thick slurpy sounds of pluff mud releasing its hold on them.

Jasper had the sense not to run that time, but that didn't stop me from hoisting him up in my arms and walking back to the house, every inch of me covered with smelly, brown goo. It took three shampooings to get the pluff out of his coat and at least an hour to clean the spattered stains from every inch of the bathroom wall, floor, and ceiling. If the mud had been red, the room would have looked like the scene of a gruesome murder.

That mud episode would not be Jasper's last attempt at freedom. In time, we learned to lock doors with more care and waited to remove his leash until every escape hatch was completely closed off. To his credit, Jasper also calmed down a bit. I'd like to think he realized this home was not too bad after all and perhaps he shouldn't be in such a hurry to leave it. Or at least, not so often. I am happy to report he's avoided marshes since that night.

For the holidays, we gave the kids a DNA kit to determine all the breeds that made up our beloved "lab mix," as the shelter had described Jasper on his adoption sheet. We were surprised to learn not only did he have no Labrador in him at all, but he was a jumbled mix of every other breed out there. While we had already suspected, his broad chest came from his pit bull genes; his exotic, almond-shaped eyes from a Chihuahua (seriously?); his wrinkled brow from a cocker spaniel. There was also some German shepherd thrown in for good measure.

*Great!* We had managed to adopt the penultimate Frankenstein, containing parts from every dog imaginable. A pit bull with a Chihuahua's attitude. That explained a lot.

And yet it didn't matter. When we walked into the Humane Society that fateful day, armed with our lengthy checklist, we ended up adopting a dog that had almost none of our must-haves. Somehow, though, he was the exact dog our family needed. Thank goodness, too, since I'm not sure any other family could have survived him. Imperfect, changeable, and neurotic like the rest of us, Jasper fits right in, and we love him all the more for it.

# Tuesday Morning's Coffee Crew

Bill Newby

Some talk finance
with notebooks, spreadsheets,
and yesterday's business pages
under their cups.

Others take turns
reading their last drafts
of memoir, story, or rhyme.

Each table surrounded,
without suits or ties.
Most in sweatshirts and jerseys,
a couple ballcaps, one beret.

Everyone's hair, a version of white.
A few in full manes,
but mostly thin whisps,
and backside bare scalps.

The coffee counter stays open,
near cakes, brownies, and muffins
artfully arranged in a chilled bright case.

One older couple camps all morning.
Laptop open. Notebook spread wide.
Moving to their favorite table
after a foursome head to their cars.

# Autumn Lesson

David Rosenberg

I scraped the first frost
off my car window this morning,
damp white powder filling my nose
and stinging my hand.
I drove the winding roads -
canopied by red, yellow, brown, and green -
drinking in the old wooden structures,
the forests, the seasonal ways
that have ruled the lives of men and women here for centuries.
Then I saw the bulldozer,
pushing away the trees and bushes,
plowing under the wild gapes,
knocking down the old, decaying barn,
like my scraper powdering the frost.
Our history sits on us, and on the earth,
like a frosty, white veneer.
The comfort it gives, the sense of place,
the continuity, as fragile as the hoarfrost.
We scrape it away, leaving ourselves naked and vulnerable,
and this we call progress.

# Collier Beach Blues

Edra (EJ) Stephens

where footprints dance upon clouds,
swaying to sounds, floating at tides door
howling haints sing hymns of death's indigo

melanin glistening against the drag,
held tight to skinfolds on juke joints sandy floor
indigo rids, upon haints slow blues

arsh hens cackled with glee, desires entry came free
ma'granny cries for ner'come yah's yanking
howling haints, hymns of death's indigo

time, before lips touched a moon so bold
shrimp boats beach'd from leaseholds due
indigo hides, upon haints slow blues

life everlasting stifled smells of pluff's undue
sweetgrass chuckled, at buckruh's stretch
howling saints, sing hymns of death's indigo

fireflies dance to salty sweetness long foretold
footsteps of shine, holding greasy white bread
howl haints of hymns at death's indigo

groove to the sounds of boohag's sadness
riding the nights slow, salty groves
howling hymns, at death's indigo,

champagne ale gone, sparkling structures stand new
what dat younder want, don't you see it come due
haints ride deaths waves to the juke joints door

*Collier Beach* | Edra Stephens

# Ruby Lee's South

LA Winkle

There's this place called Ruby Lee's
where black meets white
over a moaning saxophone
and the sweetest collard greens
in the Southeast.

It's a place where they celebrate
a couple barely swaying on the dance floor.
Been married for fifty-two years.
When it's their turn, the young bop and churn,
raucous laughter echoing off the walls.

It's a place where you drop in late
for a strong Irish Coffee
and a slice of pecan pie
laced with bourbon,
set down by a bartender named Liz.

The owners greet you like siblings.
Chat over the neighborhood news.
Today is Mahogany's birthday.
Everyone wraps her in a warm embrace.

You tap your toes,
shake your head in affirmation,
shout out a little, "Oh, yeah!"
and you feel way better here—
swinging in this club—
than swinging a club at any 'ole country club.

# I Had the Craziest Dream

Gloria Krolak

*A poem constructed of jazz tune titles.*

Marian the Librarian,
Drinking with the Queen of Bohemia,
(Orange Was the Color of Her Dress then Blue Silk)
She Lives in Brazil, For the Moment.
She Became A Thousand Birds.
Ain't That Peculiar?
The Gathering, On Green Dolphin Street, It Took Me By
Surprise,
        Angel, Another Girl, Manuel Deeghit,
        The Dry Cleaner From Des Moines,
Things Are Happening. It's Funny to Everyone But Me.
Enter the Dragon, Fire in the Forest.
Escape With the Queen of Bohemia
Into the Great Wide Open.
Flying Home, Nothing Else Matters.
Darn That Dream.

*On a Bookshelf* | Gloria Krolak

# A Funny Thing Happens Inside Quiet

Elizabeth Robin

The bird's constant song cries out, there,
for a spring companion. Fade out, and back
pulses the rush and rustle of water, a fountain
flows, softness jets interrupt. From a distance

a siren mourns. A truck rattles. A toilet gurgles
from the upstairs apartment. Then
        a hammer, in staccato
        the door, crashing cymbals
        a furnace, trombone bellow
        the roofer, crescendo call
and the crackle-slap of raining shingles.

Another bird raises the alarm. Perhaps a gator
slipped into the lagoon, on the hunt. Or it warns
of that rumbling human squadron.

There is no stillness here.

                    Honk, if you like quiet.

# Like Magic

Sharron Sypult

We were in Istanbul at the Spice Bazaar, sampling Turkish delight (one of the oldest sweets in the world), when someone with humongous hands started massaging my back. Those Herculean hands were heaven sent and made me almost forget the pistachio-date candy coated with powdered sugar.

My aching back said, "Find a fluffy pillow and relax." With no pillow in sight, I closed my eyes for a minute, maybe more, and surrendered to the rubdown and subsequent euphoria. Normally, I would have stopped those fingers from working their magic, but that's neither here nor there because the back rub was better than a frozen drink in the desert.

I thought the massage would stop. It didn't. After a fitting interval, perhaps longer, I opened my eyes. "Who is that?" I whispered to my travel buddy Sansing. (Her name rhymes with "dancing.")

"I ... DON'T ... KNOW," her lips said. She was watching like a guard dog.

At some point, I decided to break the spell. I turned and looked into the eyes of a stranger, a swarthy salesman, not a wizard, smiling down at me. He was friendly, forward, and handsy like many Turkish men we met. Some vendors even called me "honey" or "baby" or "sweet thing."

In ancient Ephesus, Russell Crowe (AN actor acting like THE actor in *Gladiator*) showed me around, his arm draped about my shoulders. He took Sansing's hand and knelt as if proposing—a photo op for vendors hawking priceless photos as we left.

In Canakkale, a carpet salesman locked the doors and wouldn't let us leave. We were on an excursion, learning about Turkish carpets, celebrated for intricate patterns and bright colors. During a handweaving demonstration, women double-knotted threads into a dense fabric. Our male guide said women weave carpets, NOT MEN, because women have "better eyesight" and "intelligent fingers." Some customers chuckled, maybe to be polite. I gave Sansing a side eye. Then I started thinking about child marriages and honor killings. Stereotypes, I know, but still!

Men served us raki, the national drink. It's made of grapes, brandy, and anise—similar to ouzo in Greece but stronger. No one told us to drink slowly.

I was savoring the taste when someone whisked Sansing away to parts unknown in a move worthy of Houdini. POOF! I searched three sprawling floors filled with carpets and buyers buying carpets, unaware of a fourth floor, but she was nowhere to be found. Sansing had wandered off to parts unknown as she was wont to do on occasion, but omigod, in Turkey? She didn't answer my texts or calls, and no one seemed to know her whereabouts.

A comfy chair with fluffy pillows near the front door called to me. I camped there in wait, hanging by a carpet thread and wondering what to do and what to make of the carpet company's hocus-pocus.

A man wearing chic chains and rings appeared, TA-DAH, and began showing me fashionable jewelry. He was a handler, and I was handed to him on a Turkish platter, minus an apple in my mouth. My handler fastened a gorgeous necklace with zultanite stones costing a mere $12,000 around my neck. Naturally, it looked divine. He said my friends would be envious. *No doubt!*

I asked, "Where IS my friend?"

He shrugged and hugged my shoulders to reassure me, but I wasn't assured.

Huggy seemed unmoved when told the necklace cost more than I wanted to spend. In a nifty sleight of hand, he slipped a stunning $1,500 bracelet with black gemstones on my wrist. He said it was one of a kind. I texted a photo to my daughter and asked if she thought the price reasonable.

After an expletive or two, she said, "NO"—or words to that effect.

Still no Sansing. I couldn't leave her inside. I couldn't get out because the doors were still locked. And when I tried "Open sesame," the doors did not open.

The showroom was clearing, and the hugs continued. Finally, I looked at Huggy with my steeliest, steely eyes and said, "I want to leave NOW! Please open the doors!"

Then and there, someone magically found Sansing. "She'll be right down," Huggy said.

I waited like a spinning-ball cursor. A relentless sales pitch followed for what seemed like a thousand and one nights, made longer by Huggy's hugs and rubs. I felt like Aladdin's lamp.

Wal-laaaaaaah! Sansing turned up as if nothing were amiss. She seemed enchanted and never mentioned her vanishing act. She was holding paperwork for a rug, a rug that took a YEAR to weave—or so they said.

"Did you buy a rug?" I asked, even though I knew the answer.

"Yes, I did!"

Sansing sat down at a table behind me to fill out forms, one to ship her rug to the States. The doors remained locked. Huggy became more animated. I was trying to disengage and escape his clutches without being an ugly American. Unbeknownst to me and before I could say "Salaam," Sansing flat-out bought a gold ring.

"Sansing," I said. "Are you seriously buying that ring?" I don't know why I even asked.

"Yes! I like it!" *Naturally!*

No preacher, timeshare salesman, or sarcasm could dissuade her, especially when the price was lowered a second time. Sansing, under some buying spell (or raki), purchased the ring lickety-split before I could whistle "Dixie." I must admit it looked rather good on her hand.

Meanwhile, Huggy reduced the price of the bracelet to $500—which gave me pause. He whispered I can't remember what and hugged me as if he'd known me for years, not hours that just seemed like years.

I wanted to leave. Immediately! After Sansing completed her purchase, and NOT before, a man at the Turkman Rug Company unlocked the doors. ABRACADABRA! We escaped with Sansing's credit card burning hot and my principles intact.

Months passed, but her rug *never* arrived. I call it a rug even though its size limited foot traffic. Oh, yeah, I forgot to mention its size: 9x12 INCH. INCH, mind you! Some rugs are not meant for walking. What's equally eye-popping is the price she paid for that little piece of Turkey: a whopping $2,000 plus tax and shipping.

After six months and no sign whatsoever of that pricey rug, Sansing disputed the $2,000-plus charge on her credit card, a dispute that worked like magic. Two weeks later, SHAZAM, the rug arrived. She had it framed and hung in her living room.

To this day, Sansing and her handwoven silk rug—perfect for a dollhouse, but not mortal feet—make me smile. I never regret anything that makes me smile. Well … almost never.

# RENEWAL

*Shell* | Tom Mills

# C. Change

David Rosenberg

Change found being fourteen difficult enough. School was a constant burden with its stupid rules, punishing teachers, and the machinations of cliques and bullies. To make it worse, Change didn't fit in at all. When other kids looked at him, he could feel their discomfort from ten feet away. As interesting as the girls were, he knew he didn't occupy a speck in their awareness unless he was being teased or bullied, and then he was either an object of pity or amusement. That he stuttered and needed to be in a wheelchair made things even worse.

His parents thought it best to "mainstream" him. They assured him he would be grateful later, that the opportunity to socialize with his peers was essential to his development. He knew they were wrong. He experienced each day as a kind of torture, like when "Big-dog" Hartigan taunted him in the lunchroom for asking for the k-k-k-k-ketchup. Worse incidents had occurred in the gym. Even Principal Froontmann was no help, especially in assemblies, with his habit of pointing out how diverse the student body was by using "Mr. Change" as an example.

But at least he had his spot. The weather was dry today, so he rolled himself across the hard dirt behind his house and just squeezed through the border of trees to the boulder that protruded from the ground not too far from the edge of the woods. It was, quite literally, his rock. Change rubbed his hands on its rough surface, touched the furry moss that grew on its side, and inhaled the fragrance of decaying leaves that surrounded it. This was the only place he would allow himself to dream.

In this wonderful solitude, with his chair rolled up against the boulder, he dreamed of small victories. He knew it was even beyond the power of God to raise his crazy body from the wheelchair, so he didn't dream of walking into school or becoming a basketball star. Instead, Change dreamed of eating lunch in the cafeteria with pretty Lynette Wilkerson (who would not suffer anyone to call her Lynn), fist bumping Big-dog and hearing him say, "What up, Change-man," and being ignored in assembly by Mr. Froontmann. These small things that seemed so beyond him were the kinds of dreams that filled him at the rock.

But on this day, Change found that he couldn't dream. Try as he might, there was only the rustle of leaves and a moment of warmth on his face as the sunlight peeked in between the gently waving branches. He thought to go back to the house but decided against it. It was peaceful enough despite his aloneness, his difference from everyone else. He tried to examine his feelings to see how deep and wide they were but felt caught in them. And then a rustling in the surrounding bushes disturbed him. He could see the tops shaking as the sound got closer until a small dog burst into a clearing on the other side of the rock. It was a Jack Russell with three legs. The dog saw him, wagged its tail furiously, ran up to him without hesitation, jumped into his lap, and began licking his face.

"Ok, good dog, good dog," Change said, pushing the dog back and examining its collar for a tag. But the dog could not contain its excitement, wriggling out of Change's hands and redoubling its efforts to lick his face. He was so occupied by the dog that he did not see the girl emerge from the woods.

"Hi," she said. "You want me to get him off you?" Change recognized her from the neighborhood. She was a high school student, a junior, he thought. She was tall with very short hair and light brown skin. Her face was pretty and kind. Her brown eyes curious, but with no sign of judgment. She wore gray sweats and running shoes and had a blue leash draped around her neck.

"No, he's ok. What's his name?"

"Rascal." They both chuckled. "I'm Vonetta," she added.

"People call me Change. That's my last name. First name is Clarence."

"Change is better. It's cool." She smiled and walked over to join him in petting the dog.

"I don't want to be rude, but what happened to his leg?" he asked.

"When he was a pup, he got hit by a car. Had to be amputated."

"Poor dog." Rascal settled in his lap, and Change stroked his head.

"Yeah, I guess. But look at him. It's hard to tell, right?" Vonetta said.

"True." Change sat thoughtfully for a moment, taking this in. "What happened to you? Oh, wait, I'm sorry, I don't mean..."

"No, it's ok. You're fine," he said. "I know I'm weird. My spine didn't form right when I was born. There's nothing they can do, so I have to be in this chair."

Vonetta looked at him for a moment, her brown eyes bringing warmth to his skin. He realized that he hadn't stuttered once since she had appeared.

"You're not weird. You and Rascal are kind of alike."

"What?"

"Like I said about Rascal. Other than your wheelchair, it's hard to tell there's anything wrong."

A squirrel leaped out of a nearby tree, landed on the boulder, and, seeing Rascal, bounded into the bushes. Rascal jumped off Change's lap to chase after it.

"I better get him," Vonetta said and turned to run after the dog. She hesitated, swiveled her head back to Change, and said, "See you again sometime." Then she ran off.

Change watched Vonetta disappear into the woods. He stared after her for a long time, feeling lighter. It occurred to him that if he wasn't in his wheelchair in this spot, he never would have talked with her. This made Change see his wheelchair as a part of him and Vonetta wasn't put off by it.

"It was my chariot," he thought. He smiled, happy that it wasn't a dream.

# My grandson Kase, Noreen, days of grief in the lines of a Sappho lyric

Skinner Matthews


Sweetheart
our grandson Kase has this infectious smile
it seems, at times, larger than the universe
                    it isn't. I imagine
only you know this as absolute.

Can you see Kase wave his little hand?
                    Hello and goodbye in the same sentence.
Nothing having left his life, he has no fear of such a thing
                                                as loss

though I am sure
                    nothing
is a place
he cannot imagine.
                    I
on the other hand
must imagine Kase
smiling at you. In my imagination
                                        this

would be the largest universe
where he
            and you
                    and I
give birth to new lives.

They spring forth, and startle Kase a bit.
                              The smallest bit
because we both know
this cannot happen
          without us being here now
who would see these lives spring forth
                              when they happen.
I am not sure we can answer this
without dying first
knowing what more there is to this life
                    we are constantly leaving.

                    I see, in the slowest wave
I imagine Kase can make, juxtapositions
                              in the smallest tender bits
                              of imagination
                              I have of you
somewhere in Heaven
                    Kase
still asking where you are.
          He knows you exist        but expects
the body of a person to respond
to his constant waves of hello and goodbye.
Thank God, only I saw the bones of your body
the letting go      your survival meant to us.
With your suffering, we wanted so much
to give you a quiet death.
                              I hope we succeeded
and you sleep with that blue blanket.
The one cousin May prayed over
more softly than any of us
                              had ever spoken.

She said the prayer as if Jesus crocheted it
love looped through her prayer
where your feather of a body will lay
softly forever    in our dreams
and heaven    that blue
white scud of a cloud
in delineation of the sky and itself
without which you cannot see
the nature of blue softness appearing

                right there.

Yes, I see now, blue softness is a tangible touch.
Our touches were so tangible and blue.

These were the last words of cousin May's prayer:
*Life, death, love and grief are the same in all languages.*
*As all Greek tragedies occur in one place*
*beauty is not missing from anywhere or anything.*

# Jack

Jeanie Silletti

Tall and manly
no hint of low birth weight,
he steps off a front porch
toward an uncertain future.

Sacred moments of farewell
yield a tender release, grandson.
A scholar surely to emerge
amidst books and mentors.

Call promised, visits few,
life beyond a homestead beckons.
Reassuring voices hide heartache,
his journey must commence.

# Come as You Are

Diane Valeri

If God had a house, and some believe She does,
the sign outside would say: *All are welcome here.*
Fragrant no-calorie, gluten-free, butter cookies would waft from
the kitchen.
Arms would outstretch to: jailbirds and cat burglars,
busy bees and lazy dogs; bookworms and litterbugs;
cuckoo birds and night owls;
bi-polar bears and local grizzlies;
poor church mice and proud peacocks.
All would be kissed, bullies would receive hugs,
predators would be wrapped in
the loving embrace they longed for.
Hitler and Gandhi would be roommates,
Athletes and couch potatoes would dance,
Trump and the Dalai Lama would tell jokes,
Disease and drama would lead a parade instead.
Taped to the entrance, a note would read:
*Come as you are. The door is open.*
No fine print
would send different colors around to the back.
No directives
would have addicts and cutters doing penance.
Rainbows would tint black-and-white ideas
with unconditional love.
All the sons and daughters,
LBGQ plus the rest of the alphabet
would share the stardust.

# Different

Susan W. Harris

*1948: Deerfield, Illinois*

I stepped off the school bus by my driveway and recalled how relieved I felt to be home. The sun glittered off the snow, and my breath became visible in the frigid air. I'd made it through another day in fourth grade. Oh, I loved my classes: English, Arithmetic, Penmanship, Illinois History, Spelling, and Music. Thursday was my favorite day when we had Library hour. If only we didn't have recess. It was the worst time of day.

I clutched my blue and gray rectangular metal lunchbox with my mittened hand. Salty, my faithful dog and best friend, came bounding toward me. Wagging his tail, he circled me, eager to receive my spelling book to carry home. His greeting was a welcome change from the unfriendliness of the girls in my class.

At our door, my mother waited to give me a quick kiss and asked, as she helped remove my boots and snow pants, "How was your day?"

"Ok," I said, unbuttoning my jacket.

In the kitchen, she emptied the leftover wax paper and uneaten carrot sticks from my lunchbox. She poured the warm milk from the thermos down the drain, giving me a disappointed look. A plate of three graham crackers sat on the table next to a glass-covered butter dish, a jar of homemade strawberry jelly, and the inevitable glass of milk. After I washed my hands in the kitchen sink, I began eating. My mother washed root vegetables taken from her huge garden this past summer. "So, dear, how was school?" she asked.

I lied, "Good," and added, "I took out a book today on the life of Louisa May Alcott."

She said, "Oh, I always loved *Little Women*." Undeterred, she asked, "Was Bonnie in school today?"

"No, I guess she was sick. I missed her." I said wistfully. "She's my best friend."

"I know, dear. I hope she feels better."

Still persevering, she asked, "Did you play any fun games in recess?"

I lied again, "Yes, we all played *Mother, May I?*" I continued, "I have a spelling test tomorrow with some really hard words."

She looked at me, started to say something, and then stopped. Instead, she said, "All right, we can work on that together after dinner."

Avoiding my mother's scrutiny, I finished my snack and asked her, "May I go ice skating for awhile?"

She knew I loved to skate and understood what it meant to me. It wasn't just the skating; it was a time to find peace. She smiled and nodded. I didn't want to tell her that the "terrible duo" hadn't chosen me or allowed their other five teammates to choose me in the game. They gathered in a group and ignored me, except for loudly mocking my name and giggling. I was left to myself, as my one friend, Bonnie, was absent. I was miserable and relieved when the bell rang to indicate that recess was over. I didn't mention this to my mother because I didn't want to worry her. Recently ill, she seemed quite old to me.

It all started in first grade. We moved from Chicago to a small town in the country. My father still worked in Chicago, thirty miles away, where he owned a candy company and drove daily.

Although our address carried the small rural town's name, Deerfield, it was five miles of corn fields away. My parents remodeled an old farmhouse into a lovely, comfortable, large home that sat on ten acres. On the property were a chicken house and a small stable.

My parents loved their rural setting and raised a few chickens and ducks. My father even tried raising five steers, which proved disastrous. They escaped from their pasture and trampled my mother's fifty prize rose bushes. Mother created a large garden and planted everything, including my least favorite, broccoli. Besides numerous dogs and cats, we even owned a fluffy pet lamb that I named, "Miss Mischief." It turns out lambs grow up to become filthy, smelly, stupid sheep

Deerfield had only seven hundred and eighty residents who lived and worked there and barely knew that thirty miles away was a huge metropolis. It was a homogeneous, White, typical 1940s small town with a blue-collar workforce of mostly farmers and employees of two small factories. Town families went back for generations. They were God-fearing people with deep Midwestern values, prejudices, and mistrust of outsiders. Presbyterian, Evangelical Lutheran, and Catholic represented the religion in the township. The town was a crossroad amid cornfields with a few stores and a small cafe where locals gathered for daily news and gossip.

When you're a child, different is not good! I sensed being different. Different is being the outsider. Different is having a new dress from Marshall Fields, not Sears Roebuck. Different is living in a large home in the country. Different is having older parents. Different is taking summer vacations in California. Different is riding in my parents' Chrysler Imperial, not a Ford pickup. Different is having a maid. Different is having Jewish friends. Different is having a funny last name.

On the first day of school, I met Miss Thompson, my new teacher, who gave me a hug. She was fresh out of Teachers College. I fell in love with her. Sensing I was scared, she took my hand and led me to my desk. I wore a new plaid cotton dress with a sash tied in back. The other girls eyed me. Bunched in a group, they all seemed to know one another and giggled. The boys were all constant motion. They kept poking each other while laughing all the time.

The small rural school had only four classrooms with two grades to a room. Miss Thompson divided her children into first and second grade, seated on opposite sides of the room. She assigned desks alphabetically, according to the student's last name, which became my initial glimpse into my embarrassing name, Whitehead. I wound up in the last row next to David Zenka, who spent our entire elementary school experience torturing me.

My class was small, with only eight girls and six boys. It soon became apparent that I was the outsider. Being shy and essentially raised an only child—my four brothers were at least fifteen years older—I didn't know how to insert myself into groups. I would stand alone by the tree outside our school at recess while watching others play. They didn't try to engage me. They all grew up together and had their "group."

One day, my teacher walked me to the playground and asked a few girls to show me the slide. Carol Richards and Donna Wickstrom seemed to be the leaders of this small band of girls.

Donna said, "You go up, and Carol will be right behind you."

The others were waiting for me at the bottom, laughing as they poked their elbows into each other's side. I cautiously climbed up the ladder's steps. I sat down on the cold steel, and I could feel a little push from Carol behind me and a tug on the sash on my dress. Down I went, feeling the pull on my sash. At the bottom, the girls were giggling, and I realized one end of my sash had ripped off from the side of my dress. At the top, Carol sat smiling, holding half of my sash. I held back my tears, but from that day on, I would never wear a dress tied in back.

I think, as compensation, my teacher tried to help me. In music class, she let me ping on the coveted triangle. She chose me to erase the blackboard. She paired me with different girls to hand out colored art paper. Unfortunately, all this further divided me even more from the group. I didn't understand why the girls felt this way. But instinctively, I retreated into myself.

As I progressed through my lower-grade years, I did find one friend, Bonnie Banner. She was the smartest girl in the class and also an only child. She lived outside the town in a wooded area. Although she grew up with all the children, she never seemed to follow the girls and their games. One day, she smiled and asked, "Would you like to sit by me in the lunchroom?" From then on, we became fast friends.

I tried to ignore the whispered giggles and secrets. Sometimes, it was impossible. In third grade, for *Show and Tell*, my nemesis, David Zenka, brought a magazine picture of a big pimple. Its flaming red ring, mounded to the center, oozed white pus. The label under it read, "Get rid of Whiteheads." He passed it around the room to the hilarity of the class.

My mother kept trying to help. On my birthdays, she invited the seven girls in my class. We'd eat the cake and play games, but afterward, I would hear them make barbed comments about my "big" house and my dolls. She even called the mothers of various girls to invite them over to our house with their daughters so I could play with them. Some were polite. However, Carol Richard's mother commented, "That's not how it's done here."

Third grade was awful. David made up a jingle, "Susie Whitehead is going to marry a blackhead and have a whole bunch of pimples!" The taunt followed me throughout the rest of my elementary school career, and sometimes, the girls chanted it at recess.

Another time in third grade, Bonnie and I retreated to an inside corner of the brick school building to play "Jacks." The ring leaders, Carol and Donna, and their followers had several basketballs. They threw the balls only inches above our heads. This was not a game of catch. Once, a ball hit me. Thankfully, the bell rang to indicate recess was over. I learned never to let myself be cornered again.

It never occurred to me to physically retaliate. My upbringing was sheltered and physical discipline never happened. I was sent to my room or deprived of privileges if I misbehaved.

Years later I learned that physical abuse lurked in the background of my two taunter's families. Police were often called concerning domestic incidents.

It was late afternoon when I left to go ice skating. My house was beside an abandoned golf course that had small hills and ponds. It was on these ponds that my little world evolved. I flung my skates over my shoulder and jammed my stocking cap on my head. Wrapping my plaid wool scarf around my face, I let only my eyes peep out.

I patted Salty on the head, who wanted desperately to go with me. "Not this time, boy. You only want to chase squirrels and rabbits." I went out the door, hearing my mother say, "Susan, be home before dark."

All alone, I carefully climbed through the barbed wire fence that bordered our property. A gray light pervaded the day, and a small wind made me glad I had my scarf over my face. Over the snowy field, up the small hill, out of sight from everything and everyone, I saw my favorite pond. It was frozen over, and the wind blew it free of snow. I plopped down in the snow, took off my boots, pulled on my extra-thick wool socks, and laced up my white figure skates.

Standing, I tentatively took a few awkward glides. Slowly getting my balance, my fantasy took hold, and I imagined myself as Sonja Henie, a champion Olympic skater. My little jumps became imagined lithe leaps. My attempts at figure eights became swirls and arabesques. I skated from my soul with no one to laugh at me, make fun of my clothes, or ignore me. Alone with myself, my small oasis became a huge arena that held cheering, adoring fans.

After a time, I became tired and drawn back into reality. Now darker and colder, I saw the first light of the full moon and realized how late it had become. The wind had died, giving away to the silence I loved. Reluctantly, I took off my skates and trudged home. As I approached the barbedwire fence, my faithful friend, Salty, frantically barked as if trying to tell me it was very late. I was afraid I would be in trouble.

Bundled in her jacket and anxiously waiting for me by the fence, my mother frowned. "Susan, you are so late. I was worried," she said as she wrapped her arms around me. About to scold me, she looked down at my face and intuitively seemed to know I'd found silent relief. She walked me into our warm, safe house.

Looking back on those grade school years, I cherish the time I spent at my small ice-skating pond and my understanding mother. It gave me a quiet reprieve that allowed me to continue at school and gain strength against the bullying. In high school, my life changed dramatically. I was bused to a large suburban high school where I had many choices of friends and different paths to explore. But through the experience of my grade school years, I gained the perspective of an outsider, which I drew upon throughout my life.

*Fish Haul* | Jonathan Chase

# Matter

Judy Bauer

I brushed matter from the corner of my eye that morning
as if it would disappear and never return.

As if the detritus, collected and dried,
had never appeared in the first place
or lapped against soft tissue in my mind.

As if our years together, you and I,
were not a jagged stream
with rapids, falls and still waters
that will someday widen and flatten at the mouth
before washing into some universal ocean.

As if it doesn't matter
when you run your fingers
in the water beside mine,
I feel the ripples, stronger than ever.

# Soulful Cleanse

Bev Moss Haedrich

Nature has a way of mending our woes
that imbalance when we feel alone, unloved,
unappreciated or defeated.

The naked branches on trees overhead
give us a moment of pause
barren limbs
that have succumbed
to the chilly nights.

Their decor dropped to a hardened floor below
to lie upon the surface of the earth,
nourishment for the tiniest
creatures beneath our feet.

Reflection in the nearby pond is as I feel.
Upside down. Turned around.
Trying to make sense of it all.

The blueness of the sky above
offers hope for better days.
A lime luna moth flits
from one pink flower to the next
and back again.

A delicate butterfly joins in,
vying for the taste of a flower's nectar.
They enter, head first, deep into the crevice
of the opened tulip-shaped petals.

I'm reminded of an old-fashioned megaphone
on a record player of long ago;
this one pink instead of antique sepia.

I walk, turn, and look up
to see my life differently.
If I can.

Barren limbs on the tree again.
But wait, what's that?
Another angle, perhaps,
amidst the same blue sky.
The freshness of an evergreen
wrapped in a thick perennial blanket
as it was
last spring and summer.

The pond, green edges
falling into the wetness,
offers thin layers to absorb.

Mirroring the crispness of above,
the rolling descent of a grassy knoll,
and the dangling golden leaves
have left me breathless.

I move closer.
The bark is spotty and the water shimmers
and glistens along its spine.

Still, the blueness of the sky beyond
provides a backdrop of beauty
and clarity.

I walk to the other side of the pond,
glance back occasionally to see
where I have been,
among the muck and beauty,
where my soul has been cleansed.

# Pura Vida - A Costa Rica Poem

Travis Taborek

I arise from sleep
to the sounds
of the symphony of nature.

I gaze at the mountain,
aware that the universe is so vast,
and my place in it, so small.

As I sip my coffee
I feel the spirit of the forest
renew my energy.

I bathe in the river,
feel the water wash over me
purifying my soul.

As I wet my lips
the sting of chiliguaro reminds me
through pain comes healing.

I nourish myself
and bask in the heartfelt care of a woman
cooking me fajitas.

I remember
even in hardship,
I'm gifted with abundance.

As I close my eyes
I feel the earth breathing
and sing with my heart,
"Pura Vida."

# The Spirit Descends

Jim Riggs

I walked away from a late lunch at Fiesta Fresh on the north end of Hilton Head Island, carrying a few chips and half a Pepsi. The dark eyes of a muscular old man sitting at a table outside the restaurant caught my attention.

"Good afternoon," I greeted the man.

"Hello," he answered. His hand reached out to shake mine. The hand was rough like sandpaper. *A working man,* I thought. His strength carried through to my forearm.

He wore a beat-up San Francisco 49ers ball cap. "Are you a football fan?" I asked.

"I played football .... I'm still very strong."

He held up his arms, flexing his muscles to display impressive biceps and triceps. They showed the solid delineation that came from days of hard work or time in the gym. He talked of his age, but I had difficulty understanding him. His rural accent was thick as if sorghum glued together his words. I'm sure he said 80, a couple of years older than me. He told me he was on his way to Savannah; he was waiting for a ride.

He reached for my hand, asking, "Can we pray together?"

"Praying is never a problem."

We closed our eyes, and he said, "Our Father, we ask that your spirit come down. Surround us today. Be with my friend and with me as we do whatever it is you would have us do. Amen."

He continued to hold my hand in his strong, rough grip. His eyes moved to a rectangle of South Carolina sky visible between the roofs of several buildings.

With his free hand, he pointed to the spot of blue.

"See that patch of blue sky and white clouds?"

I saw a baby-blue sky and some high cirrus clouds drifting across.

"That is the spirit of God blessing you, my friend. See it?"

"I see it. Thank you." I glanced at my watch, thinking about errands to run and my expected time at home. "I have a meeting. I must go. It's been good talking with you. Have a great day."

He released my hand. I walked to the parking lot and my car.

A pure-white gull flew from the sky. Then another. And then, a flock of nearly a dozen gulls descended around me. I unlocked my car door and dropped into my seat, crossing my arms and staring. My mouth opened, amazed at the blue sky and beautiful, brilliant-white birds. I was left wondering what had just happened.

I bowed my head, giving a quick prayer of thanks for the man who had prayed with me, for the spirit he had called down upon me.

# St. Thomas

Skinner Matthews

Mists rise off the waters. A thousand
gods I would never have known
rising up to say hello. In prayers
for you and I, lovers of this life
we have lived with our mothers
sons, brothers, and wives. Lords
of those minutes that have died.

They all rise off these waters today
and the green hills are greener
than any summer before. Of course
there are iguanas in the trees
cormorants on the shore, waters
so blue serenity should have
a name for them.

In this mind of mine, mermaids
from Atlantis are never far behind
and when the mists finally lift
the mermaids come, the seas are quieted
more than God himself can imagine
I hear the echoes of my prayers
my brothers, my sons, and my wife.

# Reflections

Richard Kammen

I'm sitting on my back deck looking at the tidal marsh between my home and Hilton Head Island. The first hint of summer's heat surrounds me with a trace of the humidity that will soon unrelentingly hover over the Lowcountry like a weighted blanket of moist air. A glass of Sauvignon Blanc sits on the table. Condensation bubbles and flows down the side of the glass, leaving a ring of moisture, evidence of where I have my late-afternoon drink.

In the branches of live oaks that border the marsh, resurrection ferns are turning cashew brown. There has been no rain, and until it rains, they will continue to darken and shrink, only to be reborn a cheerful green with the next storm. Below the oaks are stands of palmetto bushes. The oak and palmetto leaves wave, creating a constant, quiet whispering. Spanish moss hanging from the limbs of the oaks is a weathervane, signaling this breeze is from the north.

An egret is perched on an oak branch. He sits frozen, looking for dinner on the incoming tide. In an hour, the marsh grass, now standing tall, will be nearly invisible, and the egret will have many choices. In six hours, the tide will be gone, and the neon green marsh will emit flocks of birds leaving for home after feeding. Even after five years in this place, I marvel at the predictability and importance of the tides. A chart can tell me what time high or low tide will be this day ten years from now. I hope I am here to see it.

My mind bounces from subject to subject, a pinball among random thoughts and minor problems. A brief frisson of shame washes over me for focusing on superficial things.

But if my mind goes to less trivial events—the latest scandal, or a country that is changing into something I don't recognize—I seethe with anger and have difficulty appreciating the gifts in front of me.

I quiet my mind. I am just here, in this place, this space. I pour more wine and try not to speculate on the future. I try to be as still as the egret. I sit, feeling the breeze like the palmettos, oaks, and moss. Like the ferns, I hope for summer rain.

A hummingbird flits from side to side and deftly approaches the feeder filled with the sugar water she craves. In my mind, she looks at me, then soars briefly in salute. She returns to the feeder, wings a blur, and sips.

I am no longer drinking alone.

For both of us, life is good.

*Calm* | Lindsay Pettinicchi

# The Contributors

**Cathy Bateman**

Cathy Bateman was raised on the Chesapeake Bay in Maryland. At a very early age, she felt at home surrounded by water and wildlife. Before moving to South Carolina, Cathy lived in the beautiful Shenandoah Valley in Virginia for 17 years, enjoying the natural beauty of the mountains and the area's artistic variety of art and music. While only having lived in Bluffton for a little over a year, Cathy says she feels she's found inner peace from experiencing the beauty of the low country.

**Judy Bauer**

Judy Bauer earned an MFA in fiction writing from the University of Kansas. She won the Lawrence, Kansas 2009, Langston Hughes Award for her novel in progress, *The Hesitation of Olivia Austin.* Her short story *"Click,"* published in *Coal City Review,* was a Pushcart Nominee. *"Before You Understand—After Diane Williams"* and *"Before With Other Men If I Had Tried"* were also published in *Coal City Review.* Connect with Judy at www.judybauerwrites.com.

**Jonathan Chase**

Jonathan Chase is a photographer with over 30 years of experience who's lived in Bluffton since May 2022. Previously, he lived near Lexington, Kentucky, specializing in portraits for all occasions, including families, couples, and high school seniors; the horse community of breeders, trainers, exhibitors and riders; Interscholastic sports and local Realtors. www.jonathancchase.com/about.html.

### Hiyaguha Cohen

Hiyaguha Cohen, MFA, has won the Elaine Benson/Steinbeck Award for fiction, a Top 10 Article award from the *National Business Employment Weekly,* and a First Chapter Award in the Great Gutsy Novelist Contest 2023. She's the co-founder of the Kauai Writers Conference and author of *Boldly Live as You've Never Lived Before* (Avon Books, William Morrow), among others. Hiyaguha taught writing at the university level. When not writing, she's a psychotherapist specializing in trauma. Hiyaguha edited prose in this anthology.

### Amaury Cruz

Amaury Cruz's passion for the ocean began in the waters northeast of Havana. Inspired by Jacques Cousteau, he dreamed of joining the Calypso crew. By the early '60s, he was experiencing the weightlessness of the underwater world. In the late '80s, after buying a Nikonos III, Amaury transitioned from spearfishing to underwater photography. His award-winning photography has been featured in diving publications and galleries, including the National Gallery in Paris. A Sun City Hilton Head resident, Amaury now focuses on nature and wildlife photography.

### Barry Dickson

Barry Dickson is a retired Madison Avenue Creative Director. His poetry and prose have appeared in a variety of journals, print and online, including *North American Review, PEARL Literary Magazine, Haiku Journal, HazMat Literary Review,* and his favorite, *asininepoetry.com.* He's been a finalist for the Hearst Poetry Prize and received a Pushcart Prize "Special Mention." His work covers a range of subjects, from relationships to politics to cheeseburgers.

## Suzie Eisinger

Suzie Eisinger is a freelance writer of fiction, commentary, and local interest stories. Her articles have appeared in print and online publications, including *Hilton Head Monthly, Pink Magazine, the Daily Press,* and the *Charleston Post and Courier.* Currently, she is program director for a non-profit that helps disabled and older individuals. When she is not busy writing grants and fundraising letters, she enjoys visiting her kids at college, taking her dog on long walks, and writing the Great American Novel.

## Marty Ferris

Marty Ferris says the Lowcountry calls to her heart, and she is a frequent visitor to Hilton Head. Currently residing in north Georgia's horse country, her latest submission to IWN recalls memories of teaching on an Indian reservation in the southwestern United States.

## Jessica Goody

Jessica Goody is the author of *Defense Mechanisms* and *Phoenix: Transformation Poems.* Her writing has appeared in over one hundred publications, including *The Wallace Stevens Journal, Reader's Digest, Phantom Drift, The High Window, Bird's Thumb, The Centrifugal Eye, Event Horizon, The Dime Show Review, Third Wednesday, The MacGuffin, Harbinger Asylum,* and *The Maine Review.* Jessica won the 2016 *Magnets and Ladders* Poetry Prize. Her poem "Beachcombing" is part of the Hilton Head Poetry Trail.

## Bev Moss Haedrich

Bev Moss Haedrich is a professional speaker and workshop moderator, a writer of fiction and creative nonfiction. *Soulful Cleanse*, published here, is her first submission of poetry. Her stories have appeared in the last four IWN Anthologies and regional magazines. As a self-publishing consultant, she has brought children's books and other fiction and nonfiction projects to the marketplace for clients. Visit her online at WriteStoriesWorthSharing.com.

## Susan Harris

Susan (Sue) Harris draws on personal experiences for inspiration. She and her late husband retired from Syracuse, New York, to Hilton Head in 1998. There, she spent twenty years as a professional fundraiser, writing proposals and government grants. Her short stories are in two IWN anthologies and two *Daniel Boone Footsteps* series. She is writing a book about relatives living in the early twentieth century.

## Susan Hearty

Susan Hearty grew up with writing as a way of life. She studied Writing Seminars at Johns Hopkins University and continues to take writing courses through their Odyssey program. Her writing focuses on time and place. She currently resides in the Lowcountry but originally is a New Yorker. Montauk has always been one of her favorite places.

## David Inserra

David Inserra lives on Hilton Head Island with his wife, Ellen Titus, and their dog, Mindy. He is a member of the Island Writers Network and works at the local Unitarian Church. David has finished his first novel, the speculative thriller *In Your Own Backyard*, and has started the next steps to get it out there. He is also a musician who has written over 400 songs, most about his wife. Visit davidinserra.weebly.com.

## Eric D. Johnson

Eric D. Johnson is the author of *Run to Win* and *A Second Coming,* both available on Amazon. His poetry appears on the Hilton Head Island poetry trail and in the July edition of *Local Life* magazine. Eric's short stories have been published in several anthologies, including Maria Dowd's *Journey Into My Brother's Soul, Daniel Boone's Footsteps Twists and Turns,* and IWN's *Reflections* and *Ripples.* Eric lives with his wife Gwendolyn in Bluffton. Eric managed manuscripts for *Sea Change.*

## Rick Kammen

Rick Kammen is a retired lawyer who lives and writes in either Hilton Head or San Miguel de Allende. Two of Rick's books have been published. *Tortured Justice Guantanamo* and *Tortured Justice South Carolina* are legal thrillers that have received excellent reviews. Rick's third book, *Tortured Justice Alabama,* will be published next year.

## Julie Kimmell

Julie Kimmell has always loved taking photographs. Since moving to the Lowcountry, she says, she has seen so much vibrant beauty of the vegetation and wildlife. She enjoys using her cell phone and digital cameras to capture that beauty.

## Miho Kinnas

Miho Kinnas is a writer, translator, and poet. Her latest poetry collection is *Waiting for Sunset to Bury Red Camellias.* Her essay *Impossible Love,* about a memoir, *They Call You Dambudzo,* by German writer Flora Veit-Wild, was published in Matatu Journal (June 2024). The review of *Where Is the Mouth of That Word?* by Iranian poet Maryam Ala Amjadi is forthcoming in American Book Review (Fall 2024, University of Nebraska Press).

### Gloria Krolak

Gloria Krolak is host of *Mornin' Glory*, the only broadcast program featuring the vibraphone. She was also Poetry Editor at *Jersey Jazz*, journal of the New Jersey Jazz Society. In 2019, she created *Jazz Lines ... free verse in the key of jazz*, poetry built of jazz tune titles, beautifully illustrated by the photos of Ed Berger. Her website is www.gloriajazz.com. In January 2020, she co-produced the Jazz Vibes Showcase at the Arts Center of Coastal South Carolina. Gloria copyedited *Sea Change*.

### Phil Lindsey

Phil Lindsey is a retired accountant who writes poetry as a hobby. Originally from Illinois, he moved to Bluffton with his wife Karen in 2014. He has been published in prior IWN anthologies and *Local Life* magazine. He has a poem on the Hilton Head Poetry Trail. Phil is IWN treasurer.

### James A. Mallory

James A. Mallory writes non-fiction, fiction, essays, and poetry. *Mystery Magazine* published his short story *Gut Instinct* in December 2022. *Sea Change* is his fourth IWN anthology appearance. *The Beautiful Couple*, featured in *Ripples*, is on the Hilton Head Poetry Trail at Mitchelville. A newspaper journalist for nearly 30 years, he and his wife, Frances, moved to Hilton Head in 2015 after he retired from the Atlanta Journal-Constitution as Senior Managing Editor. *Sea Change* is his third anthology as Lead Editor.

### Skinner Matthews

Skinner Matthews lives and writes on Hilton Head Island. He hopes his poetry celebrates his working-class upbringing and sheds light on the dark places that exist, like landmines, in the streets, neighborhoods, and family households of the working class and poverty-stricken. He has been published in *Amethyst Review, As Surely as the Sun Journal, Autumn Sky Poetry, Ekstasis Magazine, Livina Press, Loud Coffee Press, Rising Phoenix Review, and Susurrus.*

## Tom Mills

Tom's photography is influenced by his biomedical research and teaching background, and a love of nature and observing people in their world. He combines aesthetics and technology with a wide range of colors, objects, and light to create images meaningful to him and others. Over 100 of his images have been published in the local media, and he teaches a variety of photography classes. His photos have received many awards from local clubs and the Augusta Photography Festival.

## Tom Moseley

Tom Moseley's been behind a camera since he was ten and hasn't put the camera down since. He has shot landscape, wildlife, air and space, portrait, and street photography and has exhibited in a gallery and a museum. The 60-plus South Carolinian lives in Bluffton with his wife Judi. He's an American by birth and a South Carolinian by the grace of God.

## Bill Newby

Bill Newby, a former HHI resident who returned to Ohio, uses poetry and prose to reflect upon daily experience. His work has appeared in *Whiskey Island, Bluffton Breeze, Ohio Teachers Write*, Palm Beach Poetry Festival's *Fish Tales Contest, Blue Mountain Review, Panoplyzine, Sixfold*, and five IWN anthologies. His poetry collections (*Sea Chests or a Carry-On, Passing Through,* and *Casting*) are available from Amazon.

## Jo Paduch

Gratitude is the foundation of Jo Paduch's biography. She appreciates the beauty and wildness of the Lowcountry and the selfless and creative people living here. She first learned of the area when she was a high school sophomore in 1968, and her family vacationed on the island. She dreamed for decades of returning to the Lowcountry for the last chapter. "And here I am with a guy I have loved for 50 years! Gratitude."

## Lindsay Pettinicchi

Lindsay Pettinicchi is an award-winning, exhibited, and published photographer. HHI is certainly a photographer's paradise, and vacationing for years on the island inspired her to study photography. While nature and wildlife photography are her passion and moving targets a specialty with her Nikon camera and Tamron 600mm lens, she has branched out to and has found similar success with commercial photography. Presently, she is a professional photographer and works for *Pink Magazine*. https://lindsaypettinicchiphotography.pixieset.com

## Jim Riggs

After a career teaching mathematics in Iowa, Jim Riggs retired to Hilton Head Island, where he enjoys the beach and writing stories. His novel *Freedom Run* drew enthusiastic reviews from readers. Current projects include a historical novel, *Fannie*, about his feisty pioneer grandmother. His stories and poems have appeared in three Island Writers Network anthologies and two from the *Daniel Boone Footsteps* series.

## Susan Diamond Riley

Award-winning author and editor Susan Diamond Riley has worked in the fields of publishing, journalism, and education for nearly 40 years. Currently residing on an island in the sea, she holds a Master of Arts Degree in Children's Literature and is a member of the Society of Children's Book Writers & Illustrators, the South Carolina Writers Association, and the Island Writers Network. She is the author of the Lowcountry-based Delta & Jax Mystery Series. Learn more at www.SusanDiamondRiley.com. She edited *Sea Change* prose.

## Elizabeth Robin

Elizabeth Robin is a retired teacher and award-winning poet who has three Finishing Line Press books, most recently *To My Dreamcatcher* (2022). Robin creates literary programs here and partnered IWN with the Office of Cultural Affairs to found the HHI Poetry Trail, a 25-station route of local poets. A Piccolo Spoleto Sundown Poet (2023), she emceed IWN open mic for eight years. She's recently in *Coast Lines, Tall Women, Ukweli,* and more: http://www.elizabethrobin.com

## Dave Rosenberg

Dave Rosenberg is a therapist and writer who lives in Bluffton. He was a co-founder and executive director of the Kauai Writers Conference in Hawaii. Dave's poems have been published in *Proteus,* the literary magazine of Southampton College. He has written extensively for corporations and educational institutions, including articles, business plans, educational materials, and online courses. He is currently working on a historical novel.

## Jeanie Silletti

Jeanie Silletti is a retired community college faculty member who taught classes in cultural anthropology in Ohio before her move to Hilton Head. She recently self-published a memoir about her twelve years in Europe: *Unexpected Sojourns, My Years Living in Spain,*

*England, and Italy.* Today, she continues her interest in education as an art docent with the Telfair Museums in Savannah. Jeanie enjoys writing, especially vignettes about growing up in a large family.

## Denise Spencer

Denise K. Spencer's passion for writing poetry and essays/micro-memoirs was built on a career involving writing in many forms. After retiring as CEO of the Community Foundation of the Lowcountry and starting PhilanTOPICS LLC, a nonprofit consultancy, her casual writing became more focused on creative pursuits and less on the articles, speeches, and white papers that came before. Several collections are in development, and her daughter and granddaughter are eagerly awaiting their autographed copies. *Sea Change* is Denise's second stint as an IWN anthology poetry editor.

## Edra Stephens

Edra Stephens is a writer whose words break barriers, weaving narratives that intersect identity, race, culture, and the human experience. Her voice, resonant like a steady drumbeat, brings a unique presence to the literary world. A Watering Hole Fellow and graduate of the University of South Carolina Beaufort, her work has been featured in various anthologies. Stephens continues to delve into and celebrate the richness of her culture, highlighting its profound impact on the broader human story.

## Sharron Sypult

Sharron Sypult is an academic gone rogue—publicly, dangerously, and finally telling her own stories. As a university professor devoted to the art of teaching, she graded a gazillion papers and honed laser-sharp editing skills. Amending the writing of others is a matter of course; amending her own is another matter. Sharron published op-eds, non-fiction in several IWN anthologies, and a memoir called

*The Wild-Horse Rider.* She silently corrects the grammar, syntax, and effective writing of others. Sharron copy-edited *Sea Change.*

## Travis Taborek

Travis Taborek is an SEO content marketing specialist. As a digital nomad, he embraces a lifestyle that blends work with a life of travel, adventure, and new experiences. When not chugging down rum punches on catamarans in the Caribbean or hiking through a Costa Rican rainforest with his friends, the tree sloths, he can sometimes be found reading his poetry to people.

## Stephen Tate

Stephen Tate's passion for photography started when he was eight years old. He purchased his first camera with paper route money and later was a high school yearbook photographer. He worked as a sportswriter and photographer in college and later flew fighters in the Air Force. His travels allowed him to capture images around the world. He entered the digital, mirrorless camera world five years ago when he moved to the Lowcountry. He is an active member of the Sun City Photography Club.

## Diane Valeri

Diane Valeri was honored by *Writer's Digest* as a national contest winner. Under the pen name Miss Marti Pants, Valeri has written ten children's books in a series called *Big Words for Little Nerds.* Her play, *The Secret,* was performed at the Jersey Shore Arts Center. She describes herself as a storyteller, seer, and scribe.

## Rick VanDette

Rick VanDette is a relative newcomer to the world of photography. As an active member of the Photo Club of Sun City Hilton Head for the past two years, Rick welcomes the opportunity to learn and grow his skills as a photographer and photo artist. Rick enjoys creating images that engage his imagination, expressing what he sees in the world around him—ideally, in an artistic way. Rick shot the *Sea Change* cover photo.

## LA Winkle

LA Winkle retired to the Lowcountry after a successful career in the non-profit sector and completed an MFA Degree in Creative Writing as her first retirement project. Her poetry, which explores the relationship between the natural environment and human emotions, has been published in numerous anthologies and magazines and is featured on the Hilton Head Island Poetry Trail. Besides writing, LA enjoys world travel, pickleball, and beachcombing with her dog, Toby. She edited poetry in this anthology.

## Kyle Zubatsky

Artist by day and writer of peculiar poems and short stories by night, Kyle Zubatsky left the Midwest for Lowcountry inspiration. Her creative perspective arises from wild adventures such as llama trekking in New Mexico and bicycling 3,000 miles cross-country. An IWN member, Kyle coordinates open mic events and is a contributor to the Hilton Head Poetry Trail. Currently, she is working on a poetry collection: *Cattywampus, Slightly Askew in the South.*

To see other books by IWN writers, go to:
https://islandwritersnetworkhhi.org/members-books/

# About the Island Writers Network

When writer Jo Williams moved to Hilton Head Island in 1999, she missed her Charlotte, NC, writers' group, so she ran an ad in The Island Packet. Eighteen people responded, and twelve attended the initial meeting. Today, Island Writers Network encourages and mentors writers of all levels both in the craft and business of writing. Membership exceeds seventy members and includes published writers, journalists, bloggers, and more.

Our writers work in all genres including fiction, non-fiction, children's literature, humor, memoir and poetry.

Notable alumni/co-founders include Kathryn Wall, author of the popular Bay Tanner mystery series (St. Martin's Press); Vicky Hunnings with three mysteries (Avalon Press); and Dee Merian, whose memoir, The Best Years of Flying (Headline Books), appeared at Book Expo America in New York City in 2010. John W. MacIlroy, award-winning author of *Whatever Happens, Probably Will,* named in "The 25 Greatest Short Stories of All Time" by *Forbes Magazine.*

IWN meets three times a month: **General Meeting** (business & program) at 5:45 p.m. on the first Monday of the month (except in July, August and Labor Day); **Open Workshop** at 7 p.m., on the third Monday of every month on Zoom; and **Open Mic**, a coffee-house format at 6:30 p.m. on the last Thursday of each month. Please see our website: www. islandwritersnetworkhhi.org for meeting locations and related events.

# Past Anthologies

*Hilton Head Island: Unpacked and Staying* - 2007
*Hilton Headings* - 2009
*Living the Dream* - 2012
*Time and Tide* - 2015
*Ebb and Flow* - 2017
*Reflections* - 2019, IWN 20th Anniversary edition
*Ripples* - 2021

Available in local shops and on Amazon.com

# Index of Contributors

Made in the USA
Columbia, SC
16 November 2024